EVERYDAY LIFE IN
ANCIENT GREECE

EVERYDAY LIFE IN ANCIENT GREECE

A SOCIAL HISTORY OF GREEK CIVILIZATION AND CULTURE, SHOWN
IN 250 MAGNIFICENT PHOTOGRAPHS, SCULPTURES AND PAINTINGS

NIGEL RODGERS

southwater

This edition is published by Southwater, an imprint of
Anness Publishing Ltd, Blaby Road, Wigston,
Leicestershire LE18 4SE
info@anness.com
www.southwaterbooks.com; www.annesspublishing.com

Anness Publishing has a new picture agency outlet for images
for publishing, promotions or advertising. Please visit our
website www.practicalpictures.com for more information.

Publisher: Joanna Lorenz
Editor: Joy Wotton
Designers: Nigel Partridge, Adelle Morris
Illustrations and maps: Peter Bull Art Studio, Vanessa
Card, Anthony Duke
Production Controller: Steve Lang

ETHICAL TRADING POLICY

PUBLISHER'S NOTE

Previously published as part of a larger volume,
The Ancient Greek World

PICTURE ACKNOWLEDGEMENTS
The Art Archive: /Gianni Dagli Orti 6b, 7b, 53t, 92t, 100t;
/Archaeological Museum Spina Ferrara/Alfredo Dagli Orti 36b;
/National Archaeological Museum Athens/ Gianni Dagli Orti 5.5,
24b, 84–5, 108b; /Musée du Louvre Paris/Gianni Dagli Orti 5.6, 19bl,
20t, 44b, 45t and b, 46b, 52b, 55b, 90t, 91t, 94–5, 102b, 104b, 107t;
/Bibliothèque des Arts Décoratifs Paris/Gianni Dagli Orti 23b, 25b;
/Agora Museum Athens/ Gianni Dagli Orti 54b, 110b; /Archaeological
Museum Cherchel Algeria/Gianni Dagli Orti 14b; /Musée Archéologique
Naples/Alfredo Dagli Orti 17t, 21t, 24t, 48t, 93b; /Museo Capitolino
Rome/Alfredo Dagli Orti 36t; /Museo Nazionale Taranto/Gianni
Dagli Orti 16tl, 26t, 39tl; /Archaeological Museum Florence/Gianni
Dagli Orti 116b; /Archaeological Museum Ferrara/ Alfredo Dagli Orti
106b; /Galleria degli Uffizi Florence/ Alfredo Dagli Orti 18b; /Acropolis
Museum Athens/Gianni Dagli Orti 5.1, 8–9, 12t, 101b; /Museo
Nazionale Palazzo Altemps Rome/Gianni Dagli Orti 11t, 119b; /Antalya
Museum Turkey/ Gianni Dagli Orti 13b; /Harper Collins Publishers
14t; /Galleria Borghese Rome/Alfredo Dagli Orti 15, 22b; /British
Museum/ Eileen Tweedy 19br, 81b; /National Gallery London/Eileen
Tweedy 20b;   /Archaeological Museum Aquileia/ Alfredo Dagli
Orti 25t; /Archaeological Museum Paestum/Gianni Dagli Orti 29t;
/Neil Setchfield 32b; /House of the Poet Menander Pompeii/Alfredo
Dagli Orti 39tr; /Archaeological Museum Volos/Gianni Dagli Orti
49b; /Jean Vinchon Numismatist Paris/ Gianni Dagli Orti 51t; /Musée
Archéologique Naples/Gianni Dagli Orti 63b, 111t; /Museo Nazionale
Romano Rome/Alfredo Dagli Orti 68t; /Archaeological Museum
Ostia/ Gianni Dagli Orti 72t; /Victoria and Albert Museum London
/Eileen Tweedy 79br; /Archaeological Museum Bari/Gianni Dagli
Orti 103b; /Archaeological Museum Delphi/Gianni Dagli Orti 105b;
/Archaeological Museum Istanbul/Gianni Dagli Orti 109t; /Archaeo-
logical Museum Alexandria/Gianni Dagli Orti 109b; /Archaeological
Museum Izmir/Gianni Dagli Orti 117t; /Kerameikos Museum,
Athens/Gianni Dagli Orti 117b; /National Museum Beirut/Gianni
Dagli Orti 118b; /Heraklion Museum/Gianni Dagli Orti 120tl.
The Ancient Art & Architecture Collection: 6t, 7t, 10t, 11b, 16tr
and b, 17b, 18t, 19t, 21b, 22t, 23t, 26b, 27b, 28t, 29b, 33t, 34t and b,
35t and b, 37b, 38b, 40tl and b, 41b, 44t, 47t, 54tr, 58b, 59t, 60b,
61b, 65b, 66t, 69t, 70t and b, 71t, 72b, 74b, 80t and b, 81tl, 82b,
83t, 87t, 88t and b, 89l and r, 90b, 92b, 93t, 96t and b, 97t, 98t
and b, 99b, 101tl, 102tl, 103t, 105t, 107b, 110tr, 112t, 113t, 114b,
115t, 116t, 123tr and b; /C.M. Dixon 86b, 100br, 112b; /Prisma
5.4, 56–7; /Ronald Sheridan 39b, 52t, 64t, 73t, 78t, 91b, 118t.
The Bridgeman Art Library: /Vatican Museums and Galleries,
Vatican City 67b; /Museo Archeologico Nazionale, Naples 79bl;
/British Museum, London 110tl; /Louvre, Paris 38t, 46t; /Private
Collection/The Stapleton Collection 53b, 76b; /© Ashmolean
Museum, University of Oxford 55t, 111b; /Musee de la
Chartreuse, Douai, France/Giraudon 64b; /Biblioteca Estense,
Modena 78b; /British Library, London, UK / © British Library
Board. All Rights Reserved 79t; /National Archaeological
Museum, Athens/Lauros/Giraudon 104t; /Palazzo Ducale,
Mantua 106t; © Bradford Art Galleries and Museums, West
Yorkshire 113b.
Alan Hakim: 122b and 123tl.
Photo12.com: /Oronoz 5.2, 27tl, 28br, 30–1, 33b, 37t, 40tr, 48b,
50t, 60t, 65t, 69b, 71b, 73b, 97b, 102tr, 120tr and b, 121t and b;
/Ann Ronan Picture Library 5.3, 12tl, 42–3, 62b, 66b, 76t, 82tl,
119t; /ARJ 10b, 28bl, 47b, 49t, 50b, 62t, 63t, 67t, 68b, 74tr, 75b,
86t, 87tl, 100bl, 108t, 115b, 124t; /JTB Photo 59b, 61t, 77b,
125t; /Oasis 32t; /Bertelsmann Lexikon Verlag 58t, 77t, 82tr.
*p. 1: Relief sculpture of horse racing. p. 2: Minoan Palace at Knossos,
Crete. p. 3: The Parthenon. Left: The Temple of Poseidon, Athens.*

CONTENTS

INTRODUCTION

As this book shows, everyday life in ancient Greece has shaped the world we live in today. Its drama, philosophy, science and, above all, its evolution of the theory of democracy have had long-lasting influence throughout history.

The ancient Greeks believed popularity and artistic excellence were compatible. Democracy in Classical Athens at its zenith in the 5th century BC involved the whole citizen body (not the whole population, but a large section of it). They voted for the building of the temples on the Acropolis, still among the most admired buildings in the world. The same ordinary citizens listened to performances of plays by Athenian playwrights and chose the prize-winners. Posterity has generally agreed with their judgements, which cannot be said of every critic.

Greek theatre was a combination of opera, ballet, musical and concert. An event of high culture, it was a political rite for the whole people. Up to 17,000 spectators could sit in the theatre in Athens. Theatre had strong religious connotations, being sacred to the god Dionysus. Gods and myths were never far from Greek life.

MAKING THE LEGENDS LIVE

Many 20th-century poets and playwrights turned to Greek mythical archetypes. W.B. Yeats often used Greek myths in his poems and majestically translated Sophocles' tragedy, *Oedipus at Colonus*. T.S. Eliot tried to revive Greek poetic drama in *Sweeney Agonistes* and *The Family Reunion*. W.H. Auden reworked Greek legends in poems such as *The Shield of Achilles* and *Atlantis* to illustrate the dilemmas facing modern humanity. The playwright Eugene O'Neill adopted the themes of the *Oresteia*, a trilogy of plays by Aeschylus, to describe the impact of the American Civil War, while Tennessee Williams recast the myth of Orpheus, the archetypal poet, for his confessional play *Orpheus Descending*. The grandest Greek legend of all, the Trojan War, fascinates Hollywood still.

THE BIRTH OF REASON

Out of the mythic background there emerged the first scientific and philosophical attempts to understand and explain the world, human and natural. Early philosophers were also scientists and mathematicians, with Thales reputedly being the first to predict a solar eclipse in 585BC. Pythagoras was a philosopher, mathematician and mystic. He traditionally discovered the theory of the triangle bearing his name and suggested that the Earth floats freely in space. It was soon realized that the Earth must be round.

Working in the Museum/Library of Alexandria, the era's intellectual powerhouse, Eratosthenes calculated the globe's circumference remarkably closely.

Above: This majestic bronze of Zeus, king of the gods, dates from c.460BC. It is one of the finest original Greek statues to have survived and was found in the sea off Euboea.

Below: The Temple of Aphaia on the island of Aegina has survived unusually intact. Built c.510–490BC and sited on a rocky hilltop, it is one of the most complete and perfect examples of a Doric temple.

Aristarchus even suggested that the Earth spins around the Sun – a suggestion too far for the age, but one that later inspired Copernicus in the 16th century. In the 2nd century BC, Euclid laid down the elements of maths in books that remained authoritative until almost 1900. In medicine, Hippocrates originated the clinical analytical approach that still underlies modern doctoring.

The Greeks invented history and philosophy also. Other cultures had shown historical and philosophical interests, but only the Greeks, uniquely free from priests and kings, could examine the past with critical freedom – *historia* actually means 'inquiry'. Only in free cities like Athens could philosophers debate the aims of human life or the nature of the cosmos. (Socrates, pushing Athenian tolerance beyond its limits, was executed, but his trial was unique in Greek history.) Little wonder that Herodotus is known as 'the father of history' or that later Western philosophy has been called 'footnotes to Plato', Socrates' greatest disciple.

ATHLETES AS HEROES

The Greeks were not just intellectuals: they also pioneered competitive sports, for 'gymnasium', 'athletics' and 'Olympics' are Greek words. The Olympic Games, the first great sporting contest, started in 776BC. It was held every four years for almost 1,200 years at Olympia in south-western Greece.

Victorious athletes, who won only a crown of olive leaves, returned home to be greeted as heroes, touched with divinity. Statue, such as the *Charioteer of Delphi* were raised to their triumphs, and sacrifices were made to them after their deaths. The suppression of the Olympic Games in AD393 symbolized the passing of ancient Greece.

ATHENS, ROME AND JERUSALEM

By the end of the 1st century BC most Greeks were living under Roman control. This loss of liberty, although resented at the time, had its compensations, for the

Romans proved willing preservers and transmitters of Greek culture. Educated Romans such as Cicero studied in Athens, and Cicero later translated much Greek philosophy into Latin.

The same adoption and adaptation shaped Roman literature and religion. Paradoxically, a religion that spoke Greek finally destroyed the world of ancient Greece. Jesus and Pontius Pilate must have talked in Greek, then the common language of every educated man across the Mediterranean world. The New Testament is written in Greek, the word *Christos* being Greek for Anointed One.

Without the impact of Hellenism, Christianity might have remained just an obscure heretical Jewish sect – as imperial Rome initially regarded it. As it grew, Christianity was deeply influenced by Plato's philosophy, propagated by two great thinkers: the heretic Origen and the saint Augustine. Rome's political collapse in the west after AD400 hardly interrupted this religious process. Athens, Rome and Jerusalem are still the triple pillars of the Western world. Christian or otherwise, we remain the heirs of Greece.

Above: The Temple of Poseidon at Sunium is superbly sited overlooking the sea. Built around 440BC by an unknown architect, it was a landmark for sailors rounding the cape as they headed for Athens.

Below: The Erechtheum, one of the temples on the Acropolis, was named after the ancestor of Theseus, the legendary king of Athens. It was completed in 405BC.

CHAPTER I

RELIGION AND MYTHOLOGY

For the Greeks, the world was filled with gods and mythical beings. Greek religion underlay all society to a degree unimaginable today in the West, but it was very different from monotheistic faiths. As polytheists, the Greeks revered many different gods. To the Olympian deities worshipped by the polis, newer gods were often added. Greek gods were anthropomorphic – having human forms, faces, virtues and foibles – even when they personified natural forces such as the sun (*helios*).

If perfect in form, most gods were far from perfect in behaviour. Homer and Hesiod, whose poems shaped Greek views of the pantheon, recounted the gods' amorous, sometimes dishonest, exploits. This divine amorality later upset philosophers but hardly worried ordinary Greeks. Religion was not a matter of dogma or revealed truth, but of the correct rites performed in public. Gods had to be honoured and placated, usually by sacrifices, or the whole polis could suffer. The gap between gods and men was not wholly unbridgeable, as the cult of the heroes (semi-divine beings) reveals. Alexander the Great was worshipped as a god even in his lifetime. Greek religion flowed into myth, but *mythos* meant not 'falsehood' but 'story' or 'tale'. Greek mythology remains among the world's richest, open to many interpretations.

Left: Three of the principal Olympian deities – Poseidon, Apollo and Artemis – from the Parthenon in Athens.

THE TWELVE OLYMPIANS

The cloud-capped peak of Mt Olympus, Greece's highest mountain, was the mythical home of the Twelve Olympians. Here the deities feasted, drank and slept with each other – or with mortals abducted from below – in palaces built by Hephaestus, the blacksmith god. Although Zeus, the thunder-wielding king of the gods, was their acknowledged lord, they were a querulous brood. In this they fittingly resembled the Greeks quarrelling and fighting on earth.

The Olympians, often called sky-gods, because they roamed through the skies (although Poseidon lived in the sea) were probably introduced by Indo-European invaders who over-ran the Aegean world *c.*2000BC. Tablets in early Mycenaean Greek of *c.*1200BC seem to show that some of the Olympians, including Zeus, Poseidon and Hera, were already being worshipped in the Late Bronze Age.

However these divine newcomers seldom displaced the older deities totally. Some of the latter were *chthonic* gods, living beneath the earth. As the myths vaguely indicate, the Olympian deities soon became the unchallenged rulers of the heavens but not always of the earth. Paganism's basic tendency anyway was to incorporate other gods into the pantheon, not to exclude them.

THE 'INHERITED CONGLOMERATE'

This inclusive tendency produced what has been called the 'inherited conglomerate', with cults superimposed on each other. Such an elastic pantheon suited popular and official needs remarkably well. Gods had different titles, depending partly on their locality but chiefly on their function.

Athena, patron goddess of Athens, was called Promachos (warrior) when depicted as a warrior outside on the

Above: The wedding of Zeus, king of the gods, to Hera, queen of heaven, guardian of marriage and an often murderously jealous wife, 470BC.

Below: Zeus and Thetis, memorably painted by the 19th-century French artist Ingres. Zeus, always highly susceptible to female charms, is being urged by the sea-nymph Thetis to help her son Achilles in the Trojan War.

GREEK AND LATIN NAMES

Greek gods today are often known by their Latin names in Western countries, for the Romans came to equate their deities with the Greek ones. Below on the right are the Roman names for the most common Greek gods.

Aphrodite	Venus
Ares	Mars
Artemis	Diana
Athena	Minerva
Demeter	Ceres
Dionysus	Bacchus
Eros	Cupid
Hades	Pluto
Hephaestus	Vulcan
Helios	Sol
Hera	Juno
Hermes	Mercury
Pan	Faunus
Persephone	Proserpine
Poseidon	Neptune
Zeus	Jupiter

(Apollo and Orpheus had the same names in both Latin and Greek.)

Acropolis but Parthenos (virgin) inside the Parthenon. Hera, Zeus' wife, was similarly patron goddess of Argos. All Greeks revered Zeus, one of whose many titles was Panhellenios (god of all the Greeks). Another was Horkios (oath-keeper). For the king of the gods, who was a gentleman despite his repeated lechery, always insisted on the sanctity of oaths.

SACRIFICES AND ALTARS

In large cities such as Athens most important gods had their own temples, shrines and altars, but in a small city such as Priene in Ionia there might be only two or three shrines. Individuals chose a god for their particular purpose at the time,

OTHER GODS

If the Olympians were the city's official gods, honoured in great festivals, other gods or cults offered individuals personal consolations. Among these was salvation beyond the grave, for mainstream religion promised no afterlife worth the name. The Orphics and the Eleusinian Mysteries were the chief mystery religions, the details of which remain to this day mysterious. But Greek religion was generally concerned with this life, not the next. Typifying Greek this-worldly attitudes were the *herms* – phallic fertility figures that stood outside many people's homes.

A god of another type was the rustic Pan, originally the god of Arcadian shepherds who became increasingly popular in Athens and several other large cities. Dionysus, only a minor god in Homer, grew during the 6th century BC into a major deity. He was patron of the newly emerging theatre, and his cult offered ecstatic and rare release to women. Otherwise much repressed, they could run wild on the mountainside every spring.

Such bacchic ecstasy was exceptional. But religion was usually a cause for celebration, be it solemn for a great deity such as Athena or Zeus, or ribald for a minor rustic god such as Pan or Dionysus in his less awesome aspects as the god of wine.

but whole cities were involved in their collective public festivals. These were as much civic as religious rites.

Of these the Panathenaea, a religious festival honouring Athena, is the most famous and became the grandest. Religious rites centred on prayers – made standing up, not kneeling – libations (offerings of wine) and sacrifices. This involved domestic animals from cockerels to bulls, but only rarely fish or game and never human beings. (Even in myth, human sacrifice was always considered an abomination by the Greeks.) Bloodless offerings – the first fruits, grains, cakes and cheese – were acceptable from poorer citizens who could not afford even a cockerel. For them, public sacrifices meant a chance to eat meat, which was a luxury for most Greeks.

The altar was the focus of worship, assuming grandiose architectural forms in rich cities like Syracuse or Pergamum. The temple itself, which housed the god's statue in holy gloom, was less important if architecturally striking. Some country shrines never had a temple.

Left: Aphrodite, the love-goddess, emerging from her bath attended by Eros, god of desire. According to Homer, she was the daughter of Zeus, but Hesiod gave a gory picture of her origins. This is a Roman copy of the bronze by the 3rd-century BC sculptor Doidalsas of Bithynia.

Below: A Roman copy of a statue of Artemis. The virginal hunter-goddess roaming the woods was associated with wild animals and girls' transition to womanhood.

ZEUS, HERA AND ATHENA
THE OLYMPIAN ROYAL FAMILY

Above: A copy of Pheidias' giant chryselephantine statue of Athena that stood inside the Athenian Parthenon. Goddess of wisdom, the arts and crafts, she was the patron goddess of Athens but was worshipped in many other Greek cities.

Three deities made up the 'royal family' of Olympus: Zeus, king of the gods; his consort Hera, goddess of marriage; and Athena, born directly from his head, goddess of the arts, wisdom and handicrafts.

ZEUS

The archetypal skyfather, whose name echoes that of Sanskrit Dyaus-Pita and Latin Jupiter, Zeus was the supreme ruler of gods and mortals, almost omnipotent. Embodying power, wisdom and majesty, he lived on Mt Olympus, from which his thunderbolts might blast his enemies. Zeus was also the father of justice and mercy, hailed as *Xenios*, protector of strangers and ultimate guarantor of law, human and divine. His own record was, however, no model of good behaviour.

The youngest son of Cronus (Saturn) who had devoured his older children fearing that they would usurp him, Zeus was hidden by his mother Rhea on Mt Ida

Above: Hera, patron goddess of Samos, shaking hands with Athena, a carving made in 403BC to celebrate the loyalty of the island of Samos to Athens even in her defeat. At Samos, the Heraion, the goddess' temple, was one of the greatest in the Greek world.

in Crete. There he was brought up by nymphs. Later, Zeus made his father vomit up his siblings, then deposed him, crushed the giant Titans and established his own rule. He divided the world with his brothers, Poseidon taking the ocean and Hades the underworld. Zeus married Hera, who was his sister, but he constantly seduced women, both divine and mortal, fathering many children.

ZEUS' CONQUESTS

Among his conquests were Leto, mother of Apollo and Artemis; Europa, whom he seduced in the form of a bull, producing Minos of Crete; Danae, to whom he appeared as a shower of gold; Leda,

Left: Reconstruction of the massive statue of Zeus made by Pheidias that was once housed in the Temple of Zeus at Olympia.

At one stage Zeus, in exasperation, hung his wife upside down from Mt Olympus. But usually Hera held her own, intervening to great effect against the Trojans in war after Prince Paris had snubbed her.

Hera was the mother of Ares, the irascible war-god, and Hephaestus, the ingenious blacksmith of Olympus. Widely revered as the goddess of childbirth and marriage, Hera was particularly honoured in Argos and on the island of Samos, where one of the largest of all Greek temples was built in her honour.

ATHENA

Born fully formed from Zeus' forehead, Athena Parthenos, the Maiden, was Zeus' most brilliant child. She was often shown with shield and spear as a warrior-goddess (*Promachos*) in Athens, whose patron she became after winning a contest with Poseidon. He had offered a spring, while she produced an olive tree, symbol of peace and plenty. Athena was goddess of wisdom, learning and the arts, but she inherited her father's pride. She intervened actively on the Achaean side in the Trojan War after being spurned by Paris, who preferred the erotic Aphrodite to her own chilly beauty. Often shown with the chthonic earth snake coiled beside her and an owl symbolizing wisdom, she also sported the hideous snake-haired aegis of Medusa, whom her protégé Perseus had slain.

The Athenians celebrated Athena as the personification of their city at their great Panathenaic Festival, but she was also worshipped in many other places. At Syracuse in Sicily a particularly fine Doric temple to Athena survives inside the existing cathedral.

Left: Reconstruction of the huge statue of Athena that once stood in the Parthenon.

Below: A statue of Zeus made in Pergamum in the 2nd century AD *during the Roman Empire, copying a presumed Greek original.*

whom he seduced as a swan, fathering Helen, whose incomparable beauty started the Trojan War; Semele, who was burnt up by Zeus revealing himself in his full glory, but whose baby Dionysus was saved; and (with Zeus in the form of an eagle) Ganymede, a beautiful Trojan princeling, who became his catamite and was cup-bearer to the gods on Olympus.

Zeus was worshipped at sites throughout Greece, especially at Olympia in the Peloponnese, where the games were held in his honour. A giant chryselephantine (gold/ivory) image of Zeus by Pheidias filled Olympia's main temple. Dodona in Epirus in the north was another major sanctuary of Zeus, famed for its oracle, which Alexander and the future emperor Augustus consulted. Some poets and playwrights spoke of Zeus in tones of almost monotheistic awe, overlooking the god's more picaresque exploits.

HERA

The sister and unwilling wife of Zeus, Hera was portrayed as enthroned beside him, the queen of Olympus, majestic rather than beautiful. She often wore a triple crown, which reveals her links with the pre-Greek Great Goddess, and was accompanied by a peacock. Her temper was famously fiery – understandably so, considering Zeus' endless love affairs. Hera did not take these calmly, constantly threatening the lives of Zeus' mistresses.

APOLLO AND ARTEMIS
THE TWINS OF DELOS

Above: Apollo, god of medicine, prophecy, science and poetry, was often portrayed naked, like most male gods, as in this rare original bronze of c.490BC.

Right: The Apollo of the Tiber *showed the god as perfectly proportioned and almost dreamily aloof. This is a marble copy of the Greek original by the Athenian sculptor Pheidias.*

Apollo and Artemis were twins, born on Delos. Their father was Zeus, their mother Leto, a titaness driven by Hera's jealousy to hide on the island. The twins proved to be very different deities.

APOLLO

Apollo is the archetypal Greek god, epitomizing reason and civilization. Called Phoebus (bright/radiant), he was later identified with the sun-god Helios. But he had many titles and attributes, including Lysios, deliverer, for he was generally a beneficent deity. Typically he was portrayed as a noble, handsome, beardless young man. His cult, very strong in Sparta, spread across the Greek world and beyond, both the Etruscans and Romans welcoming him into their pantheons. Augustus built a temple to Apollo near his palace on the Palatine in Rome.

Fed with divine nectar, Apollo when only four days old strangled (or tamed) the serpent Pytho attacking his mother. He renamed the site of the attack Delphi. It became his principal shrine, its fame surpassing even that of Delos. The serpent itself became the Pythoness priestess, uttering prophecies. For Apollo was the god of prophecy, although the answers his oracle gave were famously obscure. His own motto was "Know thyself" (*gnosi seauton*), which Socrates took to heart. Apollo's other famous injunction was "Nothing in excess", a warning few Greeks heeded. Apollo promised another oracle, the Sibyl of Cumae in Italy, immortality if she loved him. When she rejected his advances, he damned her with eternal life but not youth, for she aged horribly through the centuries.

Apollo was the god of science, medicine, music and poetry. He is often shown with his lyre or bow, being called 'far-shooting'. Every winter Apollo went north to the land of the Hyperboreans, returning with spring in a gold chariot drawn by swans or griffins. Apollo's calm, remote yet sometimes perilous divinity is illustrated by his contest with Marsyas, a satyr proud of his flute-playing who rashly competed with the god of music. Judged the loser by the muses, Marsyas was tied to a tree and flayed alive.

APOLLO'S LOVE AFFAIRS

Apollo had many, sometimes unhappy love affairs, most notably with Daphne, a nymph and daughter of the river-god

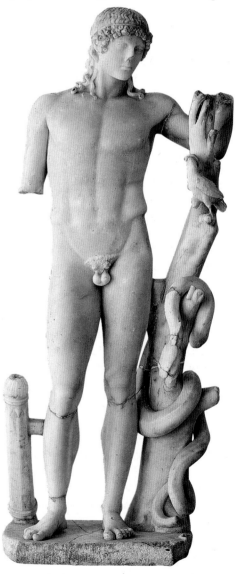

THE NINE MUSES

Apollo was at times called Apollo Musagetes (Apollo of the Muses). Seated on Mt Parnassus above Delphi by the Castalian spring of inspiration, he was shown flanked by the muses. Daughters of Zeus and Mnemosymene, these nine goddesses of poetic inspiration had, according to Hesiod, been begotten on nine successive nights. They are with their respective arts: Calliope (epic poetry); Clio (history); Erato (lyric and love poetry); Euterpe (music); Melpomene (tragedy); Polyhymnia (heroic hymns); Terpsichore (dancing); Thalia (comedy, pastoral poetry); and Urania (astronomy).

Peneus. Apollo pursued her passionately but in vain, for she prayed to her father who turned her into a laurel tree just as the god was grasping her. Another lover was the princess Coronis. When Apollo discovered she had left him, he killed her with an arrow, repenting of his anger too late. Their son Asclepius, saved by the centaur Chiron, grew up to be a divine healer. Apollo also loved Hyacinthus, a beautiful young Spartan prince, whom he taught to throw the discus. When Hyacinthus was killed by a flying discus, the hyacinth flower first sprang from the ground where his blood fell.

ARTEMIS

Apollo's twin sister, Artemis (Diana), was a paradoxical goddess. In one avatar she was the chaste hunting-goddess of the woods carrying a bow, attended by nymphs (ever-youthful and divine) whom she swore to celibacy. When a nymph Callisto, succumbing to Zeus' advances, became pregnant, Artemis changed Callisto into a bear and let the hunt dogs savage her. The hunter Actaeon, surprising Artemis and her nymphs bathing, was transformed into a stag and killed by his own hounds. As a hunting-goddess, Artemis is portrayed as tall and slim in a short skirt and carrying a bow. She had a chariot drawn by stags in this virginal woodland guise.

But Artemis was also revered as the many-breasted fertility goddess worshipped in her great temple at Ephesus, whose cult St Paul later attacked. Here she revealed a far older Asian ancestry, as the mother-goddess and Mistress of the Animals. In Classical times she presided over women's changes, most notably their transition from virgin (*parthenos*) to married woman (*gyne*). Artemis was later identified with the moon-goddess Selene, for a crescent moon was one of her symbols. The Spartans revered her as Artemis Orthia, connected with their *agoge*, their brutal education. Boys were ritually beaten at her altar in Sparta's savage initiation rites.

Below: Apollo fell in love with Daphne, but she escaped him by turning into a laurel tree. This dramatic sculpture is by Bernini (1598–1680).

POSEIDON, HERMES AND ARES

The other major Olympian gods had less in common with each other but all were larger-than-life in their power, splendour and, very often, their anger.

POSEIDON

One of Zeus' older brothers, Poseidon was swallowed by his paranoid father Cronus and then regurgitated. He fought alongside Zeus against the Titans. Subsequently allotted the sea as his realm, he ruled it with his trident, riding through the waves in a chariot drawn by *hippocampi* (sea-horses) and dolphins. Poseidon had non-marine attributes too, as the god of horses, earthquakes and springs. Like his brother, he was normally portrayed as a powerfully built, bearded older man. Like the sea, he was given to unpredictable rages. Sailors and fishermen prayed to him for a safe voyage – hence the great temple to Poseidon on Cape Sunium, visible for miles – with rich sailors sacrificing a horse. In Mycenaean times he may have been more important than Zeus, judging by tablets from Pylos, but in Classical times he was inferior to his brother.

Homer calls him *enosichthon* (earth-shaker), a potent epithet in a land as seismically active as Greece. Poseidon, who hated Odysseus for blinding his son the Cyclops Polyphemus, sealed off the port of the Phaecians with massive rockfalls for helping the wanderer. Failing to win Athens' affections in a contest with Athena, he flooded half Attica in revenge, for he was a vengeful god.

His love life was happier than many gods'. He successfully courted the Nereid (sea nymph) Amphitrite. He had seen her dancing with her sisters on Naxos when she had run away from him in alarm, but he sent dolphins to persuade her to accept him. Amphitrite then became his aquatic consort, riding beside his chariot on a dolphin or in a cockle-shell drawn by dolphins, with a retinue of other Nereids and Tritons (mermen). He rescued Amymone, a Danaid, one of the 50 daughters of King Danaeus of Argos, from a satyr pursuing her. The Isthmian Games, one of the most important in the Greek calendar, were sacred to Poseidon.

HERMES

One of the Twelve Olympians, a son of Zeus, Hermes was the eloquent messenger-god, young, graceful and swift-footed, memorably depicted by Praxiteles. Born

Above: Poseidon was Zeus' brother and a formidable god, as this bronze of the 6th century BC suggests.

Below: Poseidon, god of the sea, rides through the waves in a chariot drawn by hippocampi (sea-horses) and dolphins. From a late 2nd-century AD Roman mosaic at La Chebba, Tunisia.

Above: Hermes was the ingenious messenger-god, ferrying messages from Mt Olympus to mortals. He was also the god of shepherds, here shown as a kriophoros (carrying a ram).

to the nymph Maia in a cave in Arcadia, he was only hours old when he stole some cattle belonging to his half-brother Apollo. He managed this thanks to his divine winged sandals. By his quick wit and the timely gift of the lyre that he had invented, Hermes then saved himself from Apollo's wrath. He normally wore a broad-rimmed winged hat and carried a magic wand with two snakes entwined round it that could send people to sleep.

His ingenuity led him to be regarded as the inventor of many things, among them the alphabet, numbers and weights and measures, while his eloquence made him the patron of merchants and of thieves. As *diactoros* (messenger-god), he was constantly ferrying messages from Olympus down to earth, and he went farther down still. As *psychopompos* he led the souls of the dead down to Charon, the boatman to Hades. As the patron god of travellers, herms were set up in his honour on doors and road posts, while as *agonios* he presided over games. The Roman god Mercury took on many of his attributes.

ARES

Even his parents, Hera and Zeus, disliked Ares, the irascible red-haired god of war. The other Olympians generally shunned him too. Attended by his sons Phobos (terror) and Deimos (fear), Ares roamed the battlefields in a chariot, killing for pleasure. He was seldom victorious on the battlefield, often being outwitted by Athena or by heroes like Hercules. Nor was Ares luckier in love, with one notable exception: Aphrodite, unwillingly married to the blacksmith god Hephaestus, fell for the dashing war-god and slept with him. But their affair proved brief, for Hephaestus forged a net, which he dropped over the sleeping lovers. Ares traditionally was of Thracian origin. Despite the fact that the Greeks were often at war, and that the Areopagus, the hill facing the Acropolis in Athens, was named after him, Ares' cult was insignificant outside Thebes. But he often received sacrifices on the battlefield.

APHRODITE, EROS AND HEPHAESTUS

Above: Aphrodite, the divine embodiment of beauty and desire, here kneeling with her long hair in her hands as if she has just been bathing.

Below: Aphrodite was, according to Hesiod, born from the foam (aphros). Emerging perfectly beautiful, she was blown to land on a seashell by zephyrs, and there attended by the Horae. The myth was sublimely painted by Botticelli in c.1486.

No two deities have been less alike than Aphrodite, the beautiful goddess of love, and Hephaestus, the lame blacksmith, yet they married each other. It did not prove a match made in heaven, nor one blessed by Eros, the god of erotic love.

APHRODITE

The goddess Aphrodite, who embodied beauty, glamour and erotic allure, had disconcertingly foul origins, according to Hesiod. She was born from the foam (*aphros*) bubbling around the severed genitals of Uranus that Cronus had thrown into the sea after castrating his father. Emerging radiantly beautiful, Aphrodite was blown ashore on a seashell by zephyrs, landing at Paphos on Cyprus, which became a centre of her worship. There she was attended by three goddesses known as the Horae ('hours'), who adorned her divine nudity with jewellery and fine clothing. But Homer thought that she was simply – and more honorably – the daughter of Zeus and the minor goddess Dione.

Whatever her genesis, Aphrodite was the most desired deity on Olympus, a source of potential strife, as Zeus soon realized. He accordingly married her off to the sober Hephaestus, who made lavish jewels for her, including a magic gold girdle. But the pleasure-loving goddess, soon bored with being the wife of the industrious blacksmith god, had an affair with Ares and later with many others, both mortal and divine.

APHRODITE'S LOVE LIFE

Among her lovers was Adonis, in Greek myth the offspring of the incestuous union of King Cinyras of Paphos with his daughter Myrrha. Aphrodite fell in love with the handsome youth, but Adonis, a passionate hunter, was killed by a wild boar. Where his blood fell to earth, anemones sprouted.

Of greater legendary importance was her affair with the Trojan prince Anchises. Aeneas was their son, the Trojan who escaped from burning Troy and who, after many vicissitudes, landed in Latium to found the precursor of Rome. Julius Caesar and his imperial heirs claimed descent from Aeneas and so from the goddess.

Aphrodite won the fatal beauty contest of the Judgement of Paris. Hera, Athena and Aphrodite paraded before the dashing Trojan prince. The first two

EROS, GOD OF DESIRE

The god of desire, Eros, was the son of Hermes (or Zeus) and Aphrodite, whom he often accompanied. Shown as a boy with a bow that shot arrows of desire at his victims, Eros was thought a dangerous deity, sexual passion being considered more a sickness than a joy. Homer did not regard Eros as a proper god, but later poets such as Sappho recognized his 'bitter-sweet' powers. In contrast, Plato saw erotic desire as potentially helping to power the soul in its ascent towards the impersonal Good.

offered him respectively glory and victory but Aphrodite offered love. Paris chose love and later eloped with Helen, queen of Sparta. So started the Trojan War, in which Aphrodite provided feeble support for the Trojans, unlike Hera and Athena who vigorously helped the Greeks.

Aphrodite in origin was related to Babylonian Ishtar and Syrian Astarte, fertility goddesses, but her worship spread around the Mediterranean in Hellenized form. Aphrodite's attributes are the dove, swan and pomegranate. Besides her shrine at Paphos, she was especially worshipped at Cythera, Eryx in Sicily and at Corinth, where her devotees reputedly prostituted themselves in her temple precincts.

HEPHAESTUS

The god of fire and metal-forging, Hephaestus, could be considered the odd god out among the Olympians, being lame and ugly. His lameness came from intervening in a quarrel between his parents

Zeus and Hera, who threw him from Olympus. Falling into the sea, he was rescued by Thetis, a sea-nymph. In revenge he devised a gold throne for Hera that trapped her. Only Dionysus could persuade him to leave the sea's depths and free his mother.

In return, Hephaestus demanded the hand of Aphrodite, loveliest of goddesses. When she fell in love with Ares, the dim war-god, Hephaestus was madly jealous. He secretly forged a net of gossamer-light iron that he draped over the sleeping adulterers. They awoke trapped in it as the other Olympians gathered to laugh at them.

More usually, however, Hephaestus was kept busy at his furnace, sited beneath Mt Etna in Sicily or on Stromboli island – both active volcanoes, his Latin name being Vulcan. He built palaces for the other gods and made Achilles a magnificent shield and some armour, so memorably described by Homer, at the request of Achilles' mother Thetis. Although Hephaestus was not the most popular Olympian, the best-surviving temple in Greece is the Hephaestion on the Athenian Agora.

Left: 5th-century BC amphora showing the god of sexual desire. Eros was often shown shooting arrows of desire at his victims. He was thought to be a more dangerous than delightful deity.

Above: Aphrodite emerging from the sea attended by the Horae in an Ionian carving from the early 5th century BC.

Below: Hephaestus, the stocky god of fire and metal-forging.

DIONYSUS
THE TRANSGRESSIVE OLYMPIAN

Above: Krater showing Dionysus as an effeminate youth holding a thyrsus, a wand tipped with a pine cone.

Below: Dionysus rescuing Ariadne, abandoned on the island of Naxos, lavishly painted by Titian in 1523.

Homer hardly mentioned Dionysus, although the god's name appears on some Mycenaean tablets. But in the 6th century BC the god of wine, drama and ecstasy became one of the most important in the Greek pantheon, playing a major role in public festivals. Dionysus also offered a rare release for Greek women. One of his epithets was *eleutherios*, the liberator, for his great invention, wine, dissolved social bonds.

Dionysus thus stood in marked contrast to aristocratic Homeric gods. One of his names, Bacchus (his Roman name) was Lydian but he was no foreigner in Greece. In legend, Dionysus was the son of Zeus and Semele, a Theban princess. Urged by ever-jealous Hera, Semele rashly asked Zeus to reveal himself in his glory. When Zeus did so, she was incinerated by his intolerably manifest godhead. Zeus rescued the child she was carrying and

Dionysus was brought up by nymphs on Mt Nysa, taught by satyrs and Maenads how to make wine. When he had recovered from a fit of madness sent by Hera, he set off for India in a chariot drawn by leopards, making laws, planting vineyards, founding cities. Reurning, he married Ariadne, abandoned by Theseus on the island of Naxos. Dionysus could be a benevolent, consoling god to those who acknowledged him. To those who did not, he could be lethal, as Euripides demonstrates in his last play, *The Bacchae*.

DIONYSUS IN THEBES
When Dionysus returned from India to his native Thebes, he was welcomed by the city's people but not by its puritanical king Pentheus. The king locked up this effeminate-looking youth whose orgiastic rites affronted him. But the god mocked the

---

BACCHAE AND MAENADS
One of the most distinctive aspects of Dionysus' cult was the wild behaviour of his (mostly) female followers. Freed briefly from domestic drudgery, Greek housewives left the city for the mountains and woods to participate in Dionysiac *orgia* (secret rites or mysteries). What exactly happened in these orgies remains unclear. According to Euripides, still our best source, women known as Bacchantes got drunk and roamed the hills. Attacking wild animals with their bare hands, they daubed themselves with the blood, putting on skins torn from the still-warm beasts. In doing so they became like Maenads, Dionysus' ecstatically intoxicated worshippers. Any man who met them in their divine madness might suffer the horrifying fate of Pentheus, who was dismembered by his own raving mother.

Right: Pompeii fresco of Dionysus' keenest followers, the Maenads, women intoxicated by his worship and wine who took part in secret orgia, *ecstatic rites held outside the city.*

uptight king, but sacred ivy burst through the prison walls to free him. Then Pentheus, demented by Dionysus, dressed up as a woman to spy on the Bacchantes, the god's drunk followers celebrating on the mountains. Among them was the king's mother Agave. Also maddened by the god, Agave saw in her son a wild animal and tore him to shreds.

The moral of *The Bacchae* was that Dionysus, incarnating the forces of nature, was as unstoppable as the rising sap or melting snows. His attributes were the *thyrsus* (wand), ivy, snakes, panthers, tigers and leopards, beautiful but dangerous creatures. Usually portrayed beardless and long-haired, he was a transgressive deity, dissolving boundaries – between male and female, animal and human, man and god, one individual and the next – in mass intoxication. On Olympus, Dionysus always remained an outsider.

GOD OF THE THEATRE

Dionysus became the god of Greek theatre in the 6th century BC. Theatre started as stylized re-enactments of the god's life and death on stage. It developed into wide-ranging but still (usually) legend-based dramas. Encouraged by the Pisistratid rulers of Athens, this led after 500BC to the world's first true tragedy. Athens' three greatest playwrights, Aeschylus, Sophocles and Euripides, raised tragedy to unsurpassed heights.

There were two festivals of Dionysus in Athens. The rural Dionysia was held annually in December, a jovial procession behind a giant phallus, followed by theatrical competitions. The main event was the Greater Dionysia held in the city late in March. On this grand public holiday, the god's statue was carried in a procession to his temple on the southern Acropolis where bulls were sacrificed. Four days of dramatic competition

followed, with tragedies, comedies and satyr plays. Each playwright presented one new work in each genre, the winner receiving a crown of ivy. As patron of Athenian drama, Dionysus must rank among humanity's most beneficial deities.

Below: This mosaic from Delos shows Dionysus riding a leopard and dressed seemingly in drag, suggesting both his wildness and his sexual ambiguity.

HADES AND PERSEPHONE
GODS OF THE UNDERWORLD

Above: Demeter, Persephone and Triptolemus in a relief of the 5th century BC. Triptolemus was a prince of Eleusis to whom the goddess Demeter and her daughter Persephone, the unhappy queen of the underworld, revealed their mysteries.

Right: Hades, god of the underworld, violently abducting Persephone (Proserpine), the beautiful daughter of Demeter, goddess of corn, as passionately sculpted by Bernini in 1621.

In the three-part division of the universe that Zeus made with his brothers after they helped him to power, Hades seemingly came off worst. He got only the underworld. But what his infernal realm lacked in appeal, it made up for in horrific power. Hades, the underworld which took its ruler's name, was mentioned by the living only with huge reluctance. Hades himself was also known as Pluto, meaning wealthy, because he owned the earth's precious metals. He also grew rich on the misery of the dead, as Sophocles said. But Hades was a dim passive ruler, not an actively malevolent being.

Most Greeks anticipated a colourless, bloodless afterlife in Hades, as if in a particularly dismal retirement home. While only the notoriously wicked were actually punished by being imprisoned in Tartarus in one corner, very few even among the heroes were allowed into the delightful Elysian Fields in another area. When in *The Odyssey* Odysseus visits the underworld – making a most rare return trip – the ghosts who appear can only talk to him after he has made a blood sacrifice to give them physical substance. As Achilles' shade says, he would rather "be the most wretched slave alive on earth than a prince among the dead".

THE UNDERWORLD

Hades' realm was located underground and approached via deep caves or subterranean rivers. At its entrance lay a grove of gloomy poplars, the Grove of Persephone, and gates guarded by Cerberus. With 50 heads, each dribbling black venom, Cerberus made a formidable watchdog. Only Orpheus managed to charm the beast with his music, although Hercules overcame him by force. Once past Cerberus, the souls of the dead faced the black waters of the River Styx (or Acheron). The boatman Charon demanded an *obol* as payment. Those buried without this small coin in their mouths were left wandering forever on the desolate shores.

The Greeks were unclear about the geography of Hades, but various figures were noted there. Minos, the legendary wise king of Crete, was thought to judge the dead, but this was no Last Judgement on Christian lines, more a reckoning of accounts. Around Hades flowed the River Lethe. All who drank from its icy waters forgot their former lives.

THE ABDUCTION OF PERSEPHONE

Hades seldom left his gloomy kingdom, although he had a helmet that made him invisible when he did. His most famous

THE ELEUSINIAN MYSTERIES

The legend of the annual abduction and return of Kore ('maiden', as Persephone was first known) was central to the Eleusinian Mysteries, held in that small town near Athens. Open to everyone – male and female, free and slave – who spoke Greek and was not guilty of murder, they took place every September. A grand procession along the Sacred Way from Athens to Eleusis was accompanied by dancing and chanting. At Eleusis the neophytes bathed in the sea at nightfall and then crowded into the darkened Hall of Mysteries, the Anactorum or Telesterium. What exactly happened there is unknown – only hostile and blatantly distorted Christian accounts survive. But the rites certainly culminated in the entry of the *hierophant* (hereditary high priest) carrying a golden wheatsheaf in a blaze of light. This, symbolizing Kore's life-giving return to earth with the spring, also promised salvation after death of some sort to those initiated. The mysteries remained very popular until suppressed by the intolerant Christian emperor Theodosius I in *c*.AD395.

Finally Zeus sent Hermes down to make Hades release Persephone. Hades grudgingly agreed, but before she went back he offered Persephone a magic pomegranate. Eating it, she became bound to Hades and had to stay underground for four months each year. The other months she spent with Demeter, alongside whom she was worshipped. This division explained the earth's barrenness during winter.

As goddess of the underworld, Persephone's attributes were the bat, narcissus and pomegranate. She fell in love with Adonis, competing with Aphrodite. Zeus decreed Adonis should spend four months of the year with her in Hades.

Above: Hades carrying off Persephone in his chariot to become his unhappy queen in the underworld, as depicted on a red figure vase of c.400BC.

Below: Hades enthroned with his reluctant queen Persephone. Around them swirl the bloodless shades of the dead, forever doomed to this gloomy realm. The monstrous hound Cerberus, who guarded the gates of Hades' kingdom, can be seen just below the royal couple. From an amphora found at Canosa.

excursion led to the abduction of Persephone. The daughter of Zeus and Demeter, who was goddess of the harvest and vegetation, Persephone was so beautiful that everyone loved her, even the under-sexed Hades. One day, when Persephone was picking narcissi on the fields of Enna, Hades burst up out of the earth to carry her off in his chariot. Unwillingly Persephone became his consort, queen of the underworld. No one but Zeus and the all-seeing sun, Helios, had noticed her disappearance.

Broken-hearted, Demeter wandered the earth looking for her daughter until Helios revealed what had happened. Demeter became so angry that she withdrew her cornucopic gifts, inflicting endless drought and sterility on the earth.

PAN, HELIOS AND HERCULES

The Greeks worshipped many gods besides the Olympians. Some were rural gods like Pan. Others such as Helios (the sun) flourished during the Hellenistic period (322–30BC). Closest to most people, however, was the cult of heroes, often worshipped in their own villages.

Above: Pan and nymphs for once portrayed in an urban context at Pompeii, although the rustic god generally shunned cities.

PAN

Originally an Arcadian shepherds' god, Pan always retained his rustic air. He had the legs, horns and cloven hooves of a goat but a man's head and body. Arcadia was considered a backward part of Greece (which it was), but it was also increasingly seen as a pastoral 'arcadia' of nymphs and centaurs. Pan, son of Hermes and a nymph, was worshipped by shepherds in caves. In return he made their flocks fertile. He cavorted with nymphs, who were often alarmed by his hairy appearance but usually won over by his persistence. One exception was the nymph Syrinx. Praying for help to her father the river-god Ladon, she was changed into a reed. Pan, left clutching a bunch of reeds, consoled himself by making a flute from them, the origin of pan pipes. He also joined the wild retinue of Dionysus, seducing every Maenad he could.

"GREAT PAN IS DEAD!"

The Athenian messenger Philippides, returning through Arcadia after begging the Spartans for aid against Persia in 490BC, had a vision of Pan. The god promised to help Athens. The panic that hit the Persian forces in the Battle of Marathon was therefore

Left: Pan crouching on a rock, an unusual statue of c.200BC. Pan was said to haunt the woods and hills, especially in the deep stillness of the noonday sun.

ascribed to Pan, whom the Athenians began worshipping. (However 'panic' was originally the terror that strikes flocks in the midday heat.) Pan's name, which can mean 'all' in Greek, later led to his being worshipped as a universal deity.

His cult produced the one reported death of a pagan god. A ship sailing from Greece to Italy in the reign of the emperor Tiberius (AD14–37) heard lamentations and a voice crying: "Great Pan is dead!" However, a century later Pausanias found Pan's worship still flourishing, so reports of his death were clearly much exaggerated. Pan, quite harmless despite his appearance with horns and hooves, became for Christians the very image of the devil.

HELIOS

Although the Greeks considered Apollo the god of light, the sun had its own deity: Helios (sun). Helios was the son of the Titans Hyperion and Theca and brother of the goddesses Selene (moon) and Eos (dawn). Every morning he emerged from the eastern ocean to drive his golden chariot, pulled by dazzlingly white winged horses, across the sky, giving light to gods and men alike. At noon Helios reached his zenith and began his descent towards the west, where he appeared to plunge into the encircling Ocean. There a barque waited to carry him back east again. Zeus gave Helios the island of Rhodes and the sun-god also owned herds of oxen on the island of Thrinacia. When Odysseus' men slaughtered the 'oxen of the sun', Zeus blasted them with lightning. The Rhodians, who worshipped Helios, in the 3rd century BC raised a huge statue 30m (100ft) high to him, the Colossus of Rhodes, one of the Seven Wonders of the World. Under the Romans, Helios became generally identified with Apollo.

HERCULES, THE SUPERHERO

Midway between gods and men were the heroes. These were men, sometimes with divine parents (often Zeus and so in effect demigods), who had won undying fame. Sometimes their exploits were recounted in epic poetry and legends across the Greek world. More usually they were famous only locally, but there they were often worshipped for centuries. In Attica alone over 300 minor heroes had shrines. Only a very few, notably the muscular superman Hercules (Heracles in Greek) were Panhellenic gods.

Fathered by Zeus on the princess Alcmene, Hercules was harassed from birth by the ever-jealous Hera, who sent two snakes to kill him in his crib. The infant hero easily strangled both, however. Still madly jealous, Hera afflicted Hercules with a fit of madness, so that he killed his wife Meagre and his family. To atone for this fearful crime, Apollo ordered Hercules to perform his renowned Twelve Labours.

These tasks, regarded as utterly impossible for any normal human being, included killing the Nemaean lion, whose skin Hercules then wore, this making him almost invincible; slaying the huge Erymanthean boar and the Hydra of Lerna, a many-headed dragon; getting rid of the Stymphalian birds, which were iron-clawed man-eaters; cleaning the Augean stables fouled by 3,000 oxen; stealing golden apples from the Hesperides, the islands of the blessed; and, lastly, descending to Hades to seize Cerberus, its monstrous watchdog. All missions accomplished, Hercules became the archetypal conquering hero.

Hercules' end, however, was truly horrific. He was persuaded to wear a tunic soaked in the blood of Nessus, a centaur he had killed for trying to rape his second wife Denaira. Hercules became tormented by the poison it contained. He finally immolated himself on a pyre, but his soul ascended to Olympus. There he was deified as a constellation, like other demigods.

Right: Hercules shown wearing the skin of the Nemaean lion, one of the many creatures he had to kill as part of his Twelve Labours, in an original bronze from the 3rd century BC.

Left: The apotheosis (ascent to Olympus and deification) of the soul of Hercules the muscular superhero. From an 1813 engraving by Alexander de la Borde of an ancient Greek vase.

FESTIVALS, SACRIFICES, PRIESTHOOD AND ORACLES

Above: Consulting the oracle of Apollo at Delphi, the most revered of Greek oracles, from a vase of the 4th century BC.

Below: Sacrificial sheep being led up to the Acropolis for the Panathenaea, the great quadrennial festival, in part of a carving from the Parthenon.

Most Greek religion, closely connected with the political life of the polis, centred on festivals and sacrifices performed in public, except for mystery cults such as that at Eleusis. Public religion was generally a cheerful occasion. By celebrating their gods, citizens were celebrating their city and themselves, while public sacrifices gave poorer citizens a rare chance to eat meat. Gods were deemed content with sniffing the burnt skin and bones of sacrificed beasts.

THE PANATHENAIC FESTIVAL

Panhellenic festivals, such as the Isthmian or Olympian, were linked with their respective games attracting contestants from across Greece. More significantly,

ORACLES

Through oracles the gods spoke to men and through oracles men could ask the gods for advice and solace. The oldest known oracle in Greece was that to Zeus at Dodona in Epirus, mentioned by Homer and consulted 700 years later by the future emperor Augustus. The oracle of Zeus at Siwah in the Libyan desert later became famous, after being consulted by Alexander the Great. But Apollo was the chief oracular deity, with oracles at Didyma and Claros. All were eclipsed, however, by Apollo's oracle at Delphi, which emerged in the 8th century BC as the great Panhellenic oracle. After sacrificing a goat and paying a fee, the inquirer was admitted to the temple. There the Pythian priestess, crouched on a stool over a chasm, would enter a drugged trance. Her responses, transmitted by attendant priests, were usually in verse and always so ambiguous that they could never be proved wrong. Delphi's prestige lasted through the Roman era, the last pagan emperor Julian (AD361–3) consulting it with typically ambiguous results. It was suppressed in *c*.AD390.

each polis had its own special festivals. The Carnea was Sparta's greatest while Argos' was the Heraea, in honour of Hera, the city's tutelary goddess.

In Athens, the main festival was the Panathenaea in July. (Every four years a 'Greater Panathenea' was held.) Competitions – in music, poetry and sports – began five days before the main feast, with singing and dancing on the last night. At dawn, a sacrifice was offered to Athena and Eros, then a torch race with 40 runners carried the sacred flame to Athena's altar, high on the Acropolis.

Above: Athenians carrying vases in the great Panathenaic festival, from part of the Parthenon's renowned frieze.

At this the crowds, gathering since before dawn at the Diplyon Gate, set off in a grand procession. In front went the new *peplos* (tunic) to clothe the ancient statue of Athena Polias, the city's protector. It was carried by *arrephoroi*, four little girls chosen each year, and Athena's priestesses. More than 100 sacrificial oxen and sheep followed, with those leading them. Then came *metics* (resident foreigners), musicians, old men, military commanders and cavalry, marching in formation and carrying olive branches, and finally the rest of the city, *deme* by *deme*.

The procession moved on through the Agora and up the Acropolis, singing and chanting. In front of the little temple of Athena Nike, the best oxen were sacrificed. Only full Athenian citizens now entered the Acropolis, passing through the Propylaea to the great altar before the Erechtheum. There the little girls handed the *peplos* to the *ergastinai*, the women who had woven it, and the remaining animals were sacrificed to Athena. The ergastinai later entered the chamber of Athena Polias to change her peplos. The ceremony ended in a feast at which chosen members of each *demos* ate the sacrificed animals' meat.

This is the procession eternalized on the Parthenon carvings by Pheidias and his workshop. Here, god and heroes join idealized citizens, creating the archetypal image of Athens at its zenith in *c*.430BC. (Many sculptures are now in the British Museum.) Every fourth year from 566BC the Greater Panathenaea was celebrated with pomp as a Panhellenic festival.

PRIESTHOOD

There was no priestly caste or profession in ancient Greece. Instead, priests and priestesses were appointed from full citizens of good repute – i.e. free from blood guilt but not usually celibate. Priesthood was generally unpaid and not full-time, except at Eleusis where the priestess lived in the sanctuary. Women played an important role, serving the goddesses. Many priesthoods were normally reserved for members of noble families. The hierophant at Eleusis was chosen from the Emoulpidaie family, for example. At Sparta, the two kings took the chief priestly roles. But for local cults, the head of a local household would officiate.

Below: The theatre at Dodona in north-western Greece, dating from c.300BC. *Here, Zeus' oracle, which claimed to be the oldest in Greece, spoke through a sacred oak tree.*

Above: The Tholos, the circular sanctuary at Delphi dating from c.375BC. *The Greeks regarded Delphi with awe as omphalos, the navel of the earth.*

FUNERAL RITES AND BURIALS

Above: The Kerameikos, the main cemetery of Athens in the Classical Age, had superb funerary monuments. The city of the dead complemented the city of the living.

Below: An Athenian red figure vase depicting mourners. Dating from c.440BC and found in southern Italy, it was among Athens' many fine pottery exports.

The proper conduct of their funeral rites was always a matter of huge importance to the families concerned or, for those Greeks killed in battle, to comrades-in-arms or friends. Funeral rites determined what happened to the soul after death.

The souls of those left without the proper funeral rites were depicted by Homer in *The Iliad*, whose epics shaped all subsequent Greek religious beliefs, as forever roaming the desolate banks of the River Styx that flowed around Hades. Because of this, one way that a beaten Greek army conceded defeat was to ask permission from the victors to retrieve their dead for proper burial – a permission only rarely and most shockingly refused. (The Greeks also revered old age, and sons had by law to look after their ageing parents. But very old and infirm people were exceptional, although Sophocles lived to 90, Iscocrates to 94.)

In the Bronze Age, inhumation (burial) was apparently universal on both the islands and the mainland. The great grave-shafts of Mycenae were often superbly built structures, their many-corbelled chambers housing different members of a dynasty, the richer ones endowed with splendid grave goods. Such posthumous affluence suggests that the Bronze Age Greeks' beliefs about the afterlife may have been influenced by Egypt, as their grave architecture was.

By Homer's time, cremation had replaced burial as the normal way to dispose of the dead. In Classical times this preference for cremation continued, although inhumation was common too. In later antiquity, perhaps partly due to the rise of Christianity, inhumation once more became the norm.

FUNERALS

Relatives of the dead, usually women, carried out the elaborate three-part burial rites: the *prothesis* (exhibiting or laying out of the body), anointing the corpse with oil and dressing it in clean garments. The body was then bound in waxed cloths and put in a coffin, leaving the face uncovered. A coin was placed in the corpse's mouth to pay Charon, the ferryman who transported the dead across the River Styx into the shadow-world of Hades. The body was then placed on a

Below: For long after the funeral, women mourners made regular visits to the grave with offerings of small cakes and libations.

bier in the entrance of the house for a day before the funeral. Mourning for the dead followed, being vividly depicted on vases as early as the Geometric period.

Before sunrise the next day the body was taken out of the city in the *ekphora* (burial procession), with male relatives carrying the bier. The procession normally was led by a woman holding a libation jar. Immediately behind her came the male mourners and then all the female relatives, all wearing black or dark colours.

At times professional mourners were hired to add grandeur to the procession, with flute-players following the mourners. Aristocratic funerals could become so ostentatiously opulent that sumptuary laws were passed in many democracies, including Athens, to restrict the amount of money spent on them.

After cremation, the ashes and bones were collected in a cloth and placed in an urn, or the body was placed in a grave. Very few objects were by Classical times interred with the body, unlike the burial rites of the Bronze Age. Libations of wine and oil were then poured on to the deceased and the procession returned home. Mourners had to undergo lengthy purification ceremonies, the house itself being cleansed with sea-water and hyssop, for the Greeks believed that corpses were spiritually polluting. Later, women in mourning used to make regular visits to the grave with offerings of small cakes and libations.

FUNERAL MONUMENTS

Lavish funerary monuments were erected from the sixth century BC on by richer Athenian families in private burial grounds along the roadsides near Athens, especially on the 'Street of Tombs' in the Kerameikos quarter. This area was used for such purposes for many centuries. Relief sculpture, statues and tall *stelai* crowned by capitals marked the numerous, often sculpturally impressive, graves.

Funerary monuments often had bases inscribed with epitaphs in verse commemorating the dead. A relief depicting the dead sometimes recalled aspects of the person's life, with a favourite slave or dog. Young men killed in action were often shown fighting, idealized as heroic nudes. Many of these stelai have survived to provide vivid pictures of ancient life.

Above: A fresco of a funerary banquet from the 'Tomb of the Diver' at Poseidonia (Paestum) of c.480BC. Funerals could be scenes of ostentatious consumption.

Below: Lavish funerary monuments were erected from the 6th century BC on by richer Athenians along the 'Street of Tombs' in the Kerameikos quarter. Relief sculpture, statues and tall stelai marked many graves. Funerary monuments had inscribed bases with epitaphs commemorating the dead. Young men killed in action were depicted as fighting.

CHAPTER II

THEATRE

The Greeks produced the first tragedies and comedies still performed on stage today. Greek theatre had emerged in Athens shortly before 500BC, but its golden age lasted only 100 years. Although other dramatists wrote later, even the Greeks considered their plays relatively unimportant. Greek theatre originated in the rites of the god Dionysus, and long retained a religious aura. Highly stylized, with masked actors declaiming in verse, while a chorus chanted and danced, tragedy combined elements of opera and ballet and was normally set in a mythical past. Aristotle thought that true tragedy involved the downfall of a hero, humanly fallible, caught in a conflict with the laws of gods or men that reveal fatal character flaws. But such tragedy was never remotely mawkish. It showed adversity heroically endured or overcome, leading to resignation, even serenity. In contrast, Greek comedy offered a ribald view of the world.

Most works by the three great Athenian tragedians – Aeschylus, Sophocles and Euripides – and by Aristophanes, master of Old Comedy, are lost. Plautus and Terence, Rome's main comic playwrights, reworked Greek comedies for Roman audiences, but Roman tragedians wrote only for private readings. Roman theatre had mostly become a place of brutal thrills long before Christianity banned it. Only in the Renaissance did theatre regain its scope and humanity in the plays of Shakespeare and company. Greek theatre is the under-recognized ancestor of Western theatre, opera, musicals and even television.

Left: A red figure volute krater depicting actors preparing for a satyric drama about Dionysus and Ariadne.

PHRYNICUS AND AESCHYLUS
THE RISE OF TRAGEDY

Above: Actors on the Greek stage always wore masks, which were often very lifelike. This mask, unusual in being of gold, was perhaps made for a god's face.

Below: Tragedy was born in Athens in the 6th century BC. It reached its climax in the next 100 years with performances at the Theatre of Dionysus below the Acropolis.

Tragoidia (tragedy) originally meant 'goat-song'. It reveals Greek theatre's rustic origins in the ecstatic rites of Dionysus, who was, as god of dance, also the god of dramatic performances.

The first actors either wore goatskins or were given goats as prizes. In the mid-6th century BC, *tragoidia* came to town under the enlightened patronage of Pisistratus, Athens' tyrant or unconstitutional ruler. In 534BC Pisistratus established the Festival of the Greater Dionysia in late March, when the god's statue was carried to his temple beneath the Acropolis. There men dressed as satyrs, those mythical creatures who were half-goat half-man, danced and sang in *chorus* about the god's death and life. Soon rudimentary plays developed from these rites and drama was presented for the first time in Greece.

In 534BC the actor Thespis had made theatrical history by stepping out of the chorus and, by donning various different masks, taking different roles. Drama itself had been born. By *c.*500BC two actors were performing alongside the chorus, each one playing many parts.

PHRYNICUS c.540–c.470BC
The earliest known playwright – who also acted, like most playwrights – was Phrynicus. He won first prize for tragedy in 511BC and again for the last time in 476BC. He expanded drama by introducing female characters (played by men in masks) and by choosing serious legendary themes, not ribald subjects.

Only fragments of his plays survive. Among them are *Alcestis*, a mythical play, and two topical plays: *The Fall of Miletus* about the Persian sack of Miletus in 494BC, which proved such a painful subject for his audience (Athens had lent support to Miletus against Persia but only ineffectually) that he was fined; and his prize-winning *Phoenician Women* of 476BC. Phrynicus was most famed for his beautifully melodic verse.

AESCHYLUS c.525–456BC
Widely known as the father of Greek drama, Aeschylus was the first to write plays in trilogies, so making them suited for drama on the grandest scale. He is credited with introducing dramatic suspense, letting one character remain impressively silent, and with first employing special effects. Aeschylus himself, however, was proudest of having fought at Marathon in 490BC, according to the inscription on his tomb. (He probably also fought at Salamis.) He came from an aristocratic family, which explains this military pride, but he was no reactionary. *Eumenides*, one of his last plays, may contain radical democratic propaganda. He died in Sicily.

Aeschylus wrote 90 plays in all, winning 13 first prizes, but only seven works survive. (Some scholars doubt that

he wrote *Prometheus Bound*.) *Persian Women*, his first surviving play of 472BC, deals with the recent Persian defeat at Salamis. The play is unusually topical, not mythological, although set in the far-off Persian capital of Susa. The theme is Xerxes' despondent return, but Aeschylus does not gloat. The viewpoint is Persian and mostly female. Xerxes is the tragic hero, belatedly realizing that his own *hubris* (excessive pride) has caused his defeat.

THE ORESTEIA TRILOGY

Aeschylus' one extant trilogy is *The Oresteia*, dealing with legends of the royal house of Atreus linked to the Trojan War. It starts with *Agamemnon*, whose majestic opening lines are spoken by a watchman: "I ask the gods for relief from these pains, as I watch from one year's end to another's, Hunched on the palace roof like a dog. I have come to know the crowds of the night stars, Bright kings glimmering in the upper regions, bringing winter and summer to the earth.

I wait for the beacon light to burn, to blaze the news that the city of Troy has fallen." Troy has indeed fallen, but King Agamemnon's final homecoming brings only disaster. Clytemnestra, his wife, has long been planning his murder. Agamemnon's murder occurs offstage – the iron rule in tragedy broken only once by Euripides. The chorus, horrified, emerges finally to cry for vengance over the royal corpse.

Revenge is the theme of the next play, *Suppliants*. Orestes, Agamemnon's son, helped by his sister Electra, revenges his father by killing his mother. For this, among the worst crimes imaginable, Orestes is pursued by the Furies (*erinnyes*), hideous supernatural hags, seeking sanctuary in Delphi. In the trilogy's last play *Eumenides* (*Kindly Ones*), Orestes finally flees to Athens. There Athena judges and acquits him. She founds a new court, the Areopagus, for homicide cases, turning the Furies into the Kindly Ones, benevolent guardian spirits. (This bit may be partly propaganda for Ephialtes' democratic reforms of 458BC.)

Aeschylus called his plays "mere crumbs from Homer's table". But deep, if unconventional, religious views underlay his bold imaginative attempt to give what were often gruesome myths a firm moral basis. With him, tragedy attained an eloquent richness and simple grandeur that rival the work of Homer.

Left: Greek bust of Aeschylus. The 'father of Greek tragedy'. He was the first to write plays in trilogies, so making them suited for the highest drama.

Below: Orestes and Electra in a sculpture of the late 4th century BC. *In Aeschylus' Suppliants, the central play of The Oresteia trilogy, Orestes, Agamemnon's son, helped by Electra, revenges his father by killing his mother.*

SOPHOCLES
MASTER TRAGEDIAN c.496–406 BC

To contemporaries, Sophocles' tragedies approached perfection, a view shared by many later commentators. Aristotle thought Sophocles' *Oedipus the Tyrant* the most sublime of tragedies, the summit of all Greek drama. Sophocles' language is clearer than Aeschylus' often heavy grandeur, lacking bombast or self-conscious grandeur but retaining an epic note. His characters are roundedly human but always noble. They certainly have their faults – there would be no tragedy otherwise – but generally they conform to Aristotle's formula that tragic characters should be "like us, only finer".

Dominating Athenian theatre for almost 50 years, Sophocles had just one real rival, Euripides. Only 11 years Sophocles' junior but very different in temperament and style, Euripides wrote romances and tragicomedies besides tragedies of shocking realism. Sophocles said: "I portray men as they ought to be, Euripides shows them as they are." Sophocles' long, productive life spanned the rise and fall of the Athenian Empire, to which he contributed in many ways.

SOPHOCLES THE MAN
Born to a wealthy family at Colonus near Athens, Sophocles was a handsome youth who led the boys' chorus in victory songs after Salamis in 480 BC. Although not a politician, he had a successful public career as a Treasurer of the Athenian Empire in 442 BC, and in 440 BC served as *strategos* (general) with Pericles, his friend. Later in 412 BC, he was one of the 400 Councillors charged with drawing up a new constitution. He was markedly pious, helping introduce the cult of the healer-god Asclepius to the city in 420 BC – in effect founding a public hospital – for which he was honoured posthumously.

But Sophocles was no prig, being notorious for his love of both boys and girls. On campaign once, Pericles had to rebuke him for ogling a handsome young recruit, saying "a general must keep not only his hands clean but also his eyes". Later Sophocles joked about his declining sexual urges: "I thank old age for delivering me from a cruel master." His last public appearance in 406 BC was leading the chorus on stage in mourning for Euripides, who had just died in Macedonia.

THE PROLIFIC PLAYWRIGHT
Sophocles wrote 128 plays, winning first prize in 468 BC against Aeschylus, and on 23 later occasions. But only seven of his tragedies survive. His early style continued Aeschylus' grand manner; his middle style was more austere; his last richly expressive and dramatic. The cycle of legends connected with the Trojan War and the ill-starred royal house of Thebes supplies the material for much of his plays.

His *Ajax*, his first datable surviving play, was staged in 440 BC. In *Antigone* the heroine ignores a ban by King Creon on burying her dead brother (who had attacked Thebes), claiming a higher moral authority than the city's. This clash of

Above: Sophocles, the most prolific and arguably greatest of the three classical tragedians, in a Roman copy of an original bust of the 4th century BC.

Below: A modern performance of Sophocles' Philoctetes in the theatre at Epidaurus. Most Greek plays were performed in such open auditoria – but never at night.

Left: Oedipus and the Sphinx *painted by the French artist J.A.D. Ingres (1780–1867). The myth of Oedipus and the Sphinx has recurrently fascinated artists, writers and psychoanalysts, from Sophocles to Sigmund Freud.*

Below: Oedipus being *questioned by the man-eating Sphinx near Thebes. Answering the creature's riddles correctly saved his life but led to his doom later in Thebes. Oedipus the Tyrant is perhaps Sophocles' greatest tragedy. From a vase of the 5th century* BC.

principles leads finally to her death. *Electra* treats the same myth as Aeschylus' *Libation Bearers* but positively, for Electra's recognition of her long-lost brother Orestes brings her joy, not grief. The play is more melodrama than tragedy. In *Oedipus the Tyrant* Sophocles turned to another Theban legend. Oedipus, king of Thebes, married to Jocasta, vows to discover which god's displeasure is behind the plague ravaging the city. He consults the Delphic oracle and finally discovers that *he* is the cause. He has unwittingly killed Laius, his father, the previous king, and, married his mother. Jocasta, hearing the news, kills herself. Oedipus, learning the intolerable truth, stabs out his eyes and leaves the city. "Call no man happy until he is dead!" are the play's last lines.

A FINAL MASTERPIECE
Oedipus at Colonus, Sophocles' final masterpiece of 406BC, takes up the same story. Oedipus, now a blind, tormented vagrant, rejected by all for his horrendous crimes, arrives at Colonus in Attica. There he retells his fate to Theseus, king of Athens. Theseus accompanies Oedipus to his apotheosis, where, amid divine thunder, the old king vanishes from earth. This final play was first staged in 401BC by his grandson, Sophocles the younger.

EURIPIDES
THE LAST TRAGEDIAN c.485–406 BC

Above: Euripides, last and most controversial of the great Athenian tragedians, in a Roman copy of a Greek bust.

Below: 4th-century BC krater of Orestes with his sister Iphigenia in a scene from Iphigenia in Tauris, *a fantastical tragi-comedy written in c.412BC.*

Euripides was the last and most contro-versial of Athens' three dramatists. The least successful in his lifetime – he won only four first prizes – he became the most popular after his death. This is revealed by the high ratio of his plays to survive: 18 out of 90. Athenian captives, slaving in the mines at Syracuse after being defeated in 413BC, reputedly bought their freedom by reciting lines from Euripides' plays. With Euripides, Greek drama explored novel realms of tragi-comedy and romance before return-ing to the savage myth at its heart in *The Bacchae*. This, his final play, proved tragedy's stupendous epitaph. Aristotle called Euripides "the most tragic of poets" and he is still the most performed today.

THE DEATH OF TRAGEDY

Friedrich Nietzsche (1844–1900), the great iconoclastic philosopher and clas-sicist, blamed "Socratic scepticism" for killing Greek drama. In his *Birth of Tragedy* of 1872, Nietzsche claimed rationalism had undermined the com-munal myths that alone made Greek drama possible, turning theatre from collective rite into mere entertainment. Socrates and Euripides were the villains. While Nietzsche was the first to reveal the importance of the irrational and Dionysiac in Greek life, this view is not widely held today. Euripides knew Socrates – many Athenians did – and his plays *are* more complex than his precursors'. But Athenian society was becoming more complex and Euripides' last play, *The Bacchae*, proclaims the tri-umph of the irrational and Dionysiac. Tragedy in fact died a natural death just before the brief eclipse of Athenian democracy. The two were intertwined.

EURIPIDES THE MAN

Born on the island of Salamis (part of the Athenian state) to a respectable family, Euripides had an excellent education. He attended the lectures of Anaxagoras, Prodicus and Protagoras, three leading Sophists (itinerant teachers). A fellow-student was Pericles, who became a friend. Euripides also came to know Socrates. Aspects of Socrates' unsettling heterodoxy perhaps colour some plays.

Euripides himself was a recluse, at least by the standards of his age, retiring to Salamis to write, allegedly in a cave. More certainly, he built up one of the first book collections worth calling a library. He took almost no part in public life, unlike other playwrights. Such behaviour, unusual at the time, was mocked by

Right: A mosaic from Pompeii of the princess Medea about to kill her children before flying off in a dragon-drawn chariot in Medea, *a tragedy that won Euripides second prize when it was premièred in 431BC.*

Aristophanes. So were his radical views that portrayed women and slaves sympathetically. He was married twice, each time unhappily, and had four children.

THE INNOVATORY PLAYWRIGHT

Euripides' earliest surviving play, *Alcestis*, won second prize in 438BC. Based on folk tale, not heroic myth, it is a piquant tragicomedy, a form that the playwright made his own. *Medea*, a tragedy, also came second when staged in 431BC. It portrays the fiery barbarian princess Medea killing her rival and her own children before flying off in a dragon-drawn chariot.

His *Hippolytus* of 428BC innovates in depicting a tormented heroine. Queen Phaedra develops a disastrous passion for Hippolytus, her stepson sworn to celibacy (then most unusual). In beautiful verse, Hippolytus prays to Artemis: "Goddess, I bring you what I have created/A wreath picked from pure meadows/Where no shepherd ever pastures his flocks/Nor iron has touched, only the bees in spring…"

If reclusive, Euripides was not apolitical and *Trojan Women*, staged in 415BC after Athens had unprovokedly destroyed little Melos, highlights the fate of a captured city's women. It won him few friends in Athens at the time.

Electra in 413BC combined bitter pathos, romantic melodrama and farce in ways that still divide critical opinion, but Euripides' brilliant language captivated Athenian audiences. After the Syracusan disaster, he wrote fantastical semi-comedies such as *Helen* and *Iphigenia in Tauris*, plays with happy endings.

EXILE IN MACEDONIA

Euripides' last, and arguably greatest, play *The Bacchae* was written in Macedonia in 406BC, where he had gone at the invitation of its king, Archelaus. Returning to the sources of Greek tragedy, the play is at once beautiful in its lyric power and horrifying in its revelation of the savagely irrational in human nature.

Dionysus, god of wine and often murderous ecstasy, returns to Thebes, whose uptight king Pentheus tries to arrest him – in vain, as he breaks free. Bewitched in turn by the god, Pentheus dresses in drag to spy on the Bacchantes, which include his own mother, Agave, who, seeing in her son only a wild animal, tears him to bits, brandishing his head in gory triumph. The chorus sings chillingly at the end: "Gods have many shapes/Gods bring many things to pass./What was most expected/Has not been accomplished./But the god has found his way/For what no one expected."

Below: A Roman mosaic showing Iphigenia, daughter of Agamemnon, about to be sacrificed to Artemis in a scene from Iphigenia in Tauris.

GREEK COMEDY
ARISTOPHANES AND MENANDER

Above: The Athenians' huge respect for Aristophanes, their greatest comic playwright, was shown by pairing his head with that of Sophocles, the master-tragedian, in a double bust of the 4th century BC.

Komoidia (comedy) – another Greek word for a Greek invention – emerged around the same time as tragedy. Officially introduced to Athens' Great Dionysia in 486BC, its rustic origins are far older, going back to the seasonal ribaldry of Dionysiac fertility cults. Greek comedy divides into two phases: the Old, the often savagely topical satire of the 5th century BC; and the New, the more romantic, relaxed comedy of manners that followed. Aristophanes was the greatest but not first exponent of Old Comedy, as Menander was of the New. One of the early comedians, Cratinus (*c.*484–420BC), was Aristophanes' greatest rival, winning first prize nine times, but none of his work survives.

ARISTOPHANES C.450–385BC
Little is known of Aristophanes' early life but, although born in Aegina, he was an Athenian citizen. He wrote about 40 plays of which 11 survive. His first play, *The Banqueters*, won second prize in 427BC; his last appeared in 388BC. Although winning first prize only four times, Aristophanes aimed primarily to

make his audiences laugh. This meant catering to its often conservative feelings, but his own views were probably more liberal. He appears in Plato's *Symposium* as a friend of Socrates, whom he ridiculed in his plays. Several of his plays show unusual sympathy for women.

Aristophanes' first extant play, *The Acharnanians*, won first prize in 425BC perhaps because it voiced general war-weariness. (The Peloponnesian war had lasted six years already.) *The Knights* next year also gained first prize. It attacked Cleon, a politician whom Aristophanes portrays as an unscrupulous demagogue outwitted by an even greater scoundrel, a sausage-seller. *The Clouds* of 423BC famously depicts Socrates as an intellectual charlatan running a school of spin where young men learn to make the bad cause appear good to escape their debts. The school is finally burnt down. Seemingly unperturbed by this attack, Socrates stood up to be identified among the first audience. In *The Wasps* of 422BC Aristophanes went on to lampoon the jury courts that were supposedly filled with buzzing old men.

Below: Terracotta figurines of Greek comic actors. As in tragedy, all actors in comedies wore masks and all roles were played by men.

Above: Grotesque comic figures from a 4th-century BC vase in southern Italy.

ARISTOPHANES THE PEACEMONGER

When war resumed after 415BC, Aristophanes produced *The Birds*, an escapist story about two Athenians who, disgusted by war, go off to find somewhere better. They join up with the birds to form 'Cloudcuckooland', a fantastic utopian state hung between heaven and earth. In 411BC, as the war turned catastrophically against Athens, Aristophanes wrote *Lysistrata*. Lysistrata persuades all Greek women to refuse their husbands sex until they make peace. This has a potent effect. Finally, the Spartan envoys, similarly frustrated, arrive with peace proposals. The humour, often obscene, scarcely hides the playwright's own longing for peace. It too was to be frustrated.

Women at the Themophoria contained attacks on two tragic playwrights, the effeminate Agathon and Euripides, who had reputedly offended the women of Athens. Aristophanes' last play, *Women in Parliament*, produced in 392BC, toys with ideas of feminism and communism but his satire now lacked topical bite. Much of his wit is lost in translation – the rest is often too obscene to quote – but certain passages of pure poetry are remarkably beautiful.

Right: A Greek vase painting of a scene from Lysistrata, *Aristophanes' most political comedy, where the women of Athens refuse their husbands sex unless they make peace.*

MENANDER C.342–290BC

An Athenian of good family and friend of the eccentric tyrant Demetrius of Phalerum, Menander founded the New Comedy. After Aristophanes' death, comedy had stagnated. By adding fantastical elements from Euripides, Menander developed a new escapist form. Politics was now too grim a business for laughter, so he turned to domestic sitcoms and romances. Of his 100 plays only one, from an Egyptian papyrus, survives complete: *Dyscolus* (*The Misanthrope*). Presented at the Lenaian festival in 317BC, it won Menander first prize. In the play, a bitter but wealthy recluse violently rejects the peasant girl his son wants to marry until he falls down a well and believes he is dying. The play ends with dancing and song. Such simple plots were what now appealed. Roman comedians copied Menander so closely that New Comedy survives chiefly through their works.

Above: A Pompeii fresco of Menander, chief playwright of the New Comedy, who had a huge influence on Roman comedians and modern sitcoms.

INSIDE THE GREEK THEATRE

Above: A bronze bust of Sophocles from the 3rd century BC. By that time, the canon of the three great Athenian dramatists – Aeschylus, Sophocles and Euripides – was already firmly established.

Below: A mosaic of the 3rd century AD from Antioch, the great Hellenistic city in Syria, showing an architecturally imposing skene needed to support the scenery.

In Athens, birthplace of Greek theatre, the main dramatic performances took place during the Great Dionysia festival of late March. For four days citizens flocked to see the latest plays, with ten judges, one from each Athenian tribe, allotting prizes. In the 5th century BC plays were always new productions. But judges in the 4th century BC, realizing that newer playwrights could not compete with the great trio of tragedians – Aeschylus, Sophocles, Euripides – permitted revivals and so a classical canon emerged. While entrance cost 2 obols, an unskilled worker's daily wage, a fund provided free entry for the poorest. In the 4th century BC, women citizens too were admitted to the theatre, very probably for the first time.

Performances lasted all day, spectators sitting motionless on unpadded benches in the open, even though March can be chilly in Greece. They brought refreshments

Above: A vase showing actors holding up their masks – the one prop vital for any Greek play.

with them, eating and drinking during plays – doing so especially, Aristotle noted, if the play was poor. But theatre generally was as popular as football is today, with 15,000 or more in the audience. It was also very expensive, being closer with its masks, costumes, dancers and musicians to opera or musicals than modern theatre. In classical Athens, richer citizens, *choregoi*, were chosen to fund and put on productions personally – an onerous but honourable duty.

THE THEATRE'S STRUCTURE

By 500BC the slope below the Acropolis by the Temple of Dionysus was the site of Athenian theatre, but at first there was no theatre building. The theatre's shape derived from the orchestra (circular dancing area) for the chorus, about 25m (82ft) across, with tiers of wooden benches rising in a semicircle.

At first there was little to distract the spectator's eye from the actors and chorus, but after Persia's defeat in 479BC,

the first *skene* (background building) appeared. Xerxes' luxurious tent, captured at Plataea that year, reputedly provided the first skene (the word can mean 'tent'). Some of Sophocles' plays needed scenery, but by his debut in 468BC Xerxes' tent may have been replaced by wooden structures.

Traditionally, Pericles built Athens' first stone theatre in the 430s BC, but the oldest parts excavated are now considered 4th century BC. By 330BC, Athens' theatre had a stoa 62m (200ft) long with a colonnade facing south, away from the theatre. It served to support the skene behind it on which scenery was raised and lowered. The semicircular auditorium was now built in stone and marble.

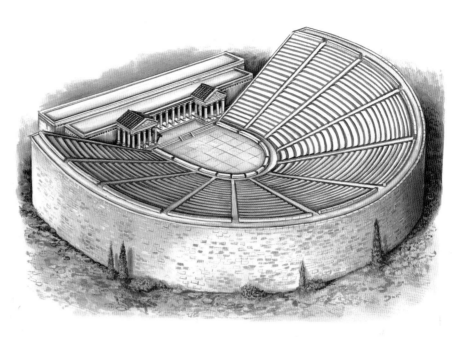

THE PERFORMERS

All actors wore masks and were male. Women were not allowed on the Greek stage. Masks were elaborate and often realistic, being made of strips of linen moulded on to the actors' faces. Some masks were horrific – one for Oedipus showed his gouged-out eyes bleeding. Aristophanes also insisted on realistic masks for the characters he was mocking, such as Socrates.

Most actors were men of good repute. A maximum of three actors played all speaking parts, making lightning-quick changes of mask and costume. Most costumes were simple, based on everyday dress. The most extravagantly dressed person on stage was the *aulos*, flute-player, who accompanied the chorus. This consisted of 12–15 actors who danced, recited and sang, but the importance of the chorus faded in the 5th century BC.

DEUS EX MACHINA

The Greeks used cranes to introduce gods from on high on to the stage and then to whisk them up again. Such cranes had

Right: Actors wearing comic masks representing a slave, a peasant and an idler respectively. In comedies, broad caricature was the norm.

to be strong. In Euripides' *Medea* the queen flies across stage in a chariot with the bodies of her dead children. Socrates in *The Clouds* goes up in a bucket to view the stars. The Greek phrase for this was, *theos ek mekhane* (Latin *deus ex machina*, god from the machine). A wheeled platform also displayed events that had occurred offstage, perhaps in a palace. It was moved into view bearing, for example, the corpse of the just murdered king Agamemnon. Greek theatre could be startlingly realistic – so much so that women in the audience were said to faint at times.

Above: An archetypal Greek theatre in the form that emerged after 400BC, with a stone-built auditorium exploiting any natural slope, and a solid skene or background with some grand architectural features.

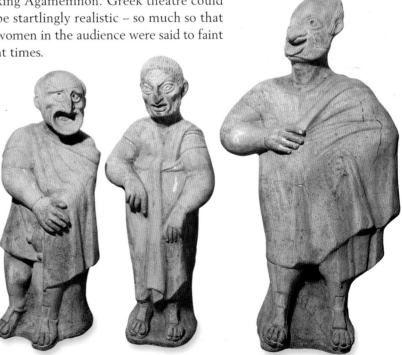

OMHPOΣ ΘΕΟΣ

ΠΕΡΣΑΙ
ΧΟΗΦΟΡΟΙ
ΑΓΑΜΕΜΝΩΝ

ΑΝΔΡΩΝ ΗΡΩΩΝ

ΚΟΣΜΗΤΟΡΙ

ΙΛΙΑΣ   ΟΔΥΣΣΕ

ΕΙ ΘΕΟΣ ΕΣΤΙΝ ΟΜΗΡΟΣ, ΕΝ ΑΘΑΝΑΤΟΙΣΙ ΣΕΒΕΣΘΩ·
ΕΙ Δ ΑΥ ΜΗ ΘΕΟΣ ΕΣΤΙ, ΝΟΜΙΖΕΣΘΩ ΘΕΟΣ ΕΙΝΑΙ

MODESTE TAMEN ET CIRCVMSPECTO IVDICIO DE TANTIS   ENDEICNYTAI HMIN O PLATWN, EI BOYLOMEQA
VIRIS PRONVNCIANDVM NE QVOD PLERISQVE ACCIDIT   MH KATWLIGWREIN WΣ KAI ANAΛH TIΣ PARA TA
DAMNENT QVAE NON INTELLIGVNT AC SI NECESSE   EIRHMENA QAOΣ EΠI TA QYHΛΑ TEINEI ΠOIA
EST IN ALTERAM ERRARE PARTEM OMNIA EORVM LEGENTIBVS   ΔE KAI TIΣ AYTH H TΩN EMΠPOΣΘEN MEΓAΛΩN

CHAPTER III

LITERATURE

Greek literature begins on an unsurpassed high. Homer, the first and grandest of Greek poets, opened *The Iliad*, his epic about the Trojan War, with the "wrath of Achilles", the archetypal warrior-hero. The poem is mainly about war, heroism and killing, described with sometimes overwhelming vividness. But the violence is balanced by passages of tenderness and humour, especially on Mt Olympus, home to oddly human gods. His second great poem, *The Odyssey*, is very different, an account of Odysseus' picaresque adventures on his slow journey home from Troy. In contrast to Homer's life-affirming gusto, Hesiod, a grumbling farmer, gave the Greeks a detailed genealogy of their gods – portrayed much less glamorously – and some sound advice, mostly on farming.

Greek literature never regained Homer's epic poetic heights, but it had no need to. Instead, it branched out over the centuries into almost every other genre, from lyric poetry to travel writing. One of the finest lyric poets was a woman, Sappho, whose fragments burn with love's bittersweetness. Many lyric poets took a lighter note, writing most unheroic verse. Others praised the triumphs of aristocratic athletes and the deeds of tyrants. The Greeks also pioneered the development of libraries. The greatest, at Alexandria, held up to 600,000 volumes. The library's destruction symbolizes the loss of Greek literature, of which only a fraction has survived. Even this has inspired later writers from the Romans to the 20th century.

Left: The Apotheosis of Homer *by J.A.D. Ingres, showing the poet honoured by other writers from Plutarch to Molière.*

HOMER, THE MASTER OF EPIC
C.730BC

Above: A bust of Homer, made long after his death in c.700BC. No actual portraits exist of the first and greatest Greek poet.

Below: Phoenix, the tutor of Achilles, being served by Briseis, the slave girl – an apocryphal scene not in The Iliad. *Homer's great epic inspired many later Greek vase-painters.*

Homer's two great epics rank among the grandest tales, in prose or verse, ever written. Although he was the very first Greek poet – or at least the first we know anything about – he is astonishingly accomplished. There is nothing crude or unformed about his two great poems: *The Iliad*, about the siege of Troy (Ilium); and *The Odyssey*, about the wanderings of Odysseus on his long journey home.

Written in hexameters (lines of six metrical feet), they were learnt by heart by every Greek school boy and frequently quoted by every adult. Homer occupied the same authoritative role as the Bible and Shakespeare once did for all English-speakers. His poetic world – of gods, heroes, beautiful women and truly regal kings – had the larger-than-life glamour and danger that Hollywood has today.

Almost nothing is known of Homer himself. He probably lived in the mid-8th century BC. He may have been " a blind man living in Chios", as the poet Semonides suggested *c.*650BC, or he may have lived in Smyrna (modern Izmir), on the Ionian coast, for his poems are in Ionian Greek, mixed with some Aeolian phrases. At one time it was questioned whether the same man had written both poems, but today most scholars think that almost certainly one man compiled both epics. Both poems make recurrent use of Homeric epithets such as "wine-dark sea", "rosy-fingered dawn", "Mycenae rich in gold" and "grey-eyed Athena". Both are huge (15,689 and 12,110 lines respectively) and depict life as seen by the age's aristocracy.

The age was Homer's own and the generations just before him (*c.*900–750BC), but garbled memories of the Mycenaean world survive. Homer incorporated fragments from much earlier poems, but his genius alone created the majestic epics of compelling drive and power. He probably wrote down nothing himself, but the revival of literacy in Greece meant that others soon did. Homer's poetry was too good to be forgotten. A definitive 'Homer' was compiled in 6th-century BC Athens.

THE ILIAD

Paradoxically, *The Iliad*, the grandest war-exulting poem, brims with life, although it starts with a murderous quarrel and ends in a funeral. The "wrath of Achilles", the finest warrior in the Achaean army besieging Troy, is stirred when Agamemnon, High King of Mycenae, demands Briseis, Achilles' favourite slave girl. From their quarrel spring the events described in this, the siege's tenth year. Achilles, sulking in his tent, refuses to fight despite disastrous Greek defeats.

Finally, Achilles' friend Patroclus goes out in his place and wearing his armour, to be killed by Hector, the Trojan prince, King Priam's eldest son. Maddened by grief, Achilles takes to the field to kill Hector in turn. Triumphing, he drags the corpse behind his chariot until Priam comes to beg in person for it. Achilles, moved, gives way, knowing that he too is doomed to die soon. The poem ends: "And so the Trojans buried Hector, tamer of horses." Still to come, as Homer's audiences knew, were the death of Achilles and the bloody final sack of Troy.

Throughout, the gods frivolously intervene to help their favourites, adding to the massacres, but the poem's carnage is tempered by other scenes. Some are tender, such as that between Hector and

land of Phaecia. At one stage Odysseus descends to the underworld to question the ghosts who flit bat-like through it.

Odysseus survives his travails more by his wits than his strength – though that is immense, as he often shows. The book culminates in his return home to Ithaca after 20 years' absence, where understandably he is not recognized at first by some of his subjects. There follows his reunion with his wife Penelope, heroically faithful to him after 20 years' absence, and meeting his now grown-up son Telemachus. Then comes his bloody reckoning with the suitors. These have long been pestering Penelope to marry one of them, for the kingdom will go to whoever marries the seemingly widowed queen.

The Odyssey ends in connubial joy in the great bed that Odysseus long ago built for Penelope. Women, human and immortal, play prominent roles throughout *The Odyssey*, which is not, like *The Iliad*, so dominated by blood-mad heroes. But the fast-moving gusto and magnificence of the poem as a whole remain truly Homeric.

Left: Odysseus blinding the giant Polyphemus, a scene from Homer's second poem The Odyssey *on a 5th-century* BC *black-figure vase.*

Below: King Agamemnon's envoys arrive to demand the slave girl Briseis from Achilles, so firing the latter's implacable wrath, which forms the central theme of The Iliad. *From a 5th-century* BC *vase made by the potter Hieron.*

his wife Andromache, with their little boy screaming in fright at the sight of his tall father in armour; some are resplendent, such as the description of Helen, as breathtakingly beautiful as ever, or of Achilles' elaborate god-forged shield: "Here youths and girls…danced and danced, arm in arm…the girls wore light flowing robes, crowned with fresh garlands, the youths had golden knives swinging from silver belts." However, such peaceful interludes are rare.

THE ODYSSEY

The second great epic opens with Odysseus, the Greek leader "who excels all men in wisdom", held captive by Calypso, the "bewitching nymph", until Athena, his champion, intervenes to liberate him. Very different in theme, it relates Odysseus' wanderings around the limits of the then-known world, and his encounters with cannibalistic giants, lethal sirens, shipwrecking monsters and finally an enchanting princess in the delightful

HESIOD'S DARK GODS
C.700BC

Above: Athena's birth from the head of Zeus shown on a 6th-century BC vase. A story told in Hesiod's poem Theogony.

Below: Hesiod's Works and Days *includes the tale of Pandora, whose box released sorrow into the world. Painted by Jean Cousin, 1540.*

Hesiod is traditionally seen as Homer's opposite as a poet and man. He has been considered a hide-bound peasant who wrote gloomily about the gods' gory origins in his *Theogony*, and a farmer's almanac interspersed with moralizing in *Works and Days*. Certainly Hesiod could be pessimistic. He describes his home near Mt Helicon in Boeotia, central Greece as "a bad place in winter, sultry in summer, good at no season of the year".

Yet Hesiod was not just a parochial old grumbler. He seems to have ended life as a substantial farmer, while his father had migrated from Cyme in Ionia. However, Hesiod totally lacks Homer's aristocratic splendour and range. His gods are not all-too-human immortals living in palaces on Mt Olympus, but ominous, sometimes inchoate creatures of the night. But his view of the underside of creation, and detailed accounts of the gods' origins, exercised an influence on later Greek religion second only to Homer's. Hesiod's dark gods aptly complement Homer's sublime deities.

Hesiod claimed to have become a poet after an encounter on Mt Helicon with the Muses, who breathed divine inspiration into him. He then went on to win a tripod in a poetry competition on Euboea. Like Homer, Hesiod wrote in hexameters but his have been called "hobnailed" by comparison.

Hesiod probably lived around 700BC but scholars remain divided as to whether one man wrote both major poems. Stories that he met and competed with Homer can be discounted, but he too wrote in Ionian if with some Boeotian phrases.

EVA PRIMA PANDORA

THEOGONY

Hesiod's first poem, *Theogony*, on the genealogy of the gods, runs to 1,022 lines. After invoking the Muses, he starts by describing "Chaos" – meaning empty space, not disorder – from which sprang night and Gaia, earth. Uranus (Heaven) emerges next – there is no creator god – and his coupling with Gaia produces more gods, including Cronus and inchoate figures called simply Night and Dreams. Encouraged by his mother Gaia, Cronus castrates his father and devours his own children to avert a prophecy that they will overthrow him. But his wife Rhea tricks him by giving him a stone to swallow instead of Zeus, their youngest son. Zeus, after growing up in Crete, forces his father to disgorge his siblings. The divine brothers then join in war against the Titans and establish the Olympian hierarchy.

After listing at a length that soon becomes tedious the other gods and demigods – including Athena, born directly from Zeus' head, and Aphrodite, the love-goddess born from the foam of Uranus' severed genitals – Hesiod ends with another invocation of the Muses. Zeus is the real hero of the poem, whose omniscience, power and justice are repeatedly stressed. Babylonian and Akkadian creation myths possibly influenced Hesiod's cosmogony.

WORKS AND DAYS

The "works" of the title of this poem are the operations of the farmer's working year; the "days" are the astrologically lucky or unlucky days of the lunar month. The poem starts by berating his feckless and greedy brother Perses, who wants more than his due share of their inherited land. It continues by describing the descent of the world from the first Age of Gold under Cronus, when men lived peacefully, to the current Age of Iron, marked by endless strife. This explains why human life is now so cursedly hard. It must, however, be born with dignity. Above all, men must work hard all their lives.

Below: Aesop's fable of the fox and grapes from a French 15th-century woodcut. Aesop's fables, once thought of minor merit, remain very popular.

Hesiod continues with farming advice that can be both sensible and poetic. "When the Pleiades, Atlas' daughters, start to rise/Begin your harvest; plough when they go down." He discourages Perses from trying to better his lot by trade, emphasizing the perils of the seas and the shortness of the sailing season – which amounts to only 50 days in his not very well informed view.

Among such brotherly admonitions come surprisingly beautiful versions of the tale of the Hawk and the Nightingale and Pandora's Box. The poem ends with a list of auspicious or lucky days.

OTHER POEMS

Some poems once attributed to Hesiod are now attributed to other writers, probably from the 6th century BC. *The Catalogue of Women* continues the *Theogony* in five books, with extensive genealogies with frequent notes, some of them on papyrus fragments recently found in Egypt. *The Shield* is a short narrative poem about Hercules' fight with Cycnus, so-called because of the detailed description of Hercules' shield with which the book starts.

Below: Cronos Devouring his Children, *one of Hesiod's darkest myths, painted by Francisco de Goya (1746–1828).*

DRINK, LOVE AND WAR
LYRIC POETS c.650–550 BC

Above: A girl with a writing tablet and stylus from a mural in Pompeii, once thought to be a portrait of Sappho.

Below: Sappho and Alcaeus, the two great poets of Lesbos, shown on a 5th-century vase.

Tiring of heroic epics, poets of later generations took a very different view of life as the Greek world revived culturally and economically. This led to new types of poetry in the Ionian or Aeolian cities and islands of the east Aegean, then probably the most developed parts of Greece. The poetry written about life in these cities was humorous, passionate and personal, very seldom heroic. Only a few of these lyric poems – intended to be sung to a lyre at *symposia* (dinner parties) – have survived, but these give us glimpses of an aristocratic, debonair yet passionate life.

ARCHILOCHUS (c.680–630 BC)

The illegitimate, penniless son of a nobleman of Paros and a slave girl, Archilochus had to leave home young. He became a mercenary, finally dying in battle against the Naxians. But his was hardly a tragic life, as his poems attest. "Some lucky Thracian has my fine shield./ I had to flee and dropped it in a wood./But I got right away, thank God!/Damn the shield, I'll find another just as good." Such insouciance, unthinkable for a Homeric hero (or a Spartan), typified the carefree aspect of the new age. Writing in a vernacular version of the Ionic dialect, he turned a keenly satirical eye on the aristocrat-ruled world. Unlike earlier poets, he freely expressed his own views, often using metaphors drawn from folklore. His sometimes savage but always original genius was recognized in antiquity.

SAPPHO (BORN c.630 BC)

The first – and only – Greek woman poet of note, Sappho was born into the aristocracy of Mytilene on the island of Lesbos. Exiled to Sicily as the result of a coup, she returned to establish not so much a school as a circle for young girls, which she dominated by her personality, anticipating Socrates' circle later in Athens. For some girls she wrote poems about the love that she may well have felt for them, giving rise to the (modern) term Lesbian.

All Sappho's poems, which survive only in the briefest fragments, concern erotic passion, although Sappho was married and had a daughter herself. Some of her poems celebrate her girls' forthcoming marriages. (The tale of Sappho leaping to her death from a cliff after being rejected by Phaeon, a male lover, is a later fiction.) Sappho wrote in the relatively obscure Aeolic dialect, not the canonical Ionic, which may explain her subsequent neglect by Hellenistic

Left: Sappho playing her lyre, theatrically imagined by the artist Léopold Burthe in 1849. Lyric poets are so-called because they accompanied their recitals on the lyre.

ALCAEUS (BORN C.620BC)

Another aristocratic poet of Mytilene who wrote in the Aeolic dialect was Alcaeus. A friend or acquaintance of Sappho, he fought as a young man for his city against Athens at Sigeum. He then became actively involved in factional politics, first as an ally and then as an enemy of Pittacus, the reforming "tyrant" who finally exiled Alcaeus and other nobles. Alcaeus visited Egypt and probably became a mercenary in the Lydian army. He was finally allowed home by 580BC, but was never reconciled to the new regime – for snobbish reasons as much as anything, it seems.

Alcaeus lived, fought and drank hard. He seems to have been better at hating than loving. This is reflected in his scathing political poetry. He wrote love poems – not just about his own affairs, which were mostly with boys, but also as the dramatic monologues of a lovesick girl – and cheerful drinking songs such as: "We should not abandon our hearts to despair/ For we gain nothing by groaning./ Bycchis, the best cure for us now/ Is to pour out the wine and start drinking".

and Byzantine scholars. (Some further fragments were discovered on papyrus scrolls in Egypt in the 1920s. Papyrus is well preserved in the desert sands.)

Whatever their subject, the intensity of Sappho's feelings fires her imagination to a white-hot passion never since surpassed. She wrote with deceptive simplicity, often in 4-line verses, couplets or even single lines. About one girl she wrote: "She outshines all the women of Lydia/As sometimes the rosy-fingered moon outshines all the stars, When its light spreads over the salt sea/ And over the many flowered fields, where the roses are blooming." Or, writing even more simply, perhaps about her own romantic loss: "The Pleiades are set/And here I Sappho lie alone."

Such poetry, despite so much being lost in translation, often has something of the heart-piercing beauty of Mozart's most lyrical arias. Catullus in the 1st century BC wrote poems that are almost exact Latin renderings of Sappho. Through his verse, which has mostly survived, Sappho came to influence the mainstream of European love poetry.

Below: Much lyric poetry celebrated symposia, here recalled on the funerary stele of Menelaus from Demetrias in Macedonia.

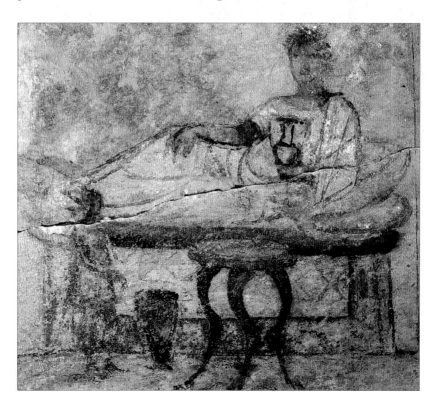

TYRANTS AND ATHLETES
THE LATER LYRIC POETS C.570–C.440BC

The advance of Persian power to the Aegean in the 540s BC meant the loss of Ionian liberty, but it did not harm lyric poets, who proved very adaptable. Most were happy to write for (Greek) tyrants and democracies. Some, like Pindar, preferred aristocratic oligarchies.

ANACREON C.570–485BC

Typical of the adaptable poet was Anacreon. Born on the small island of Teos, he followed other Teans who migrated to Abdera in the Hellespont (Dardanelles) rather than accept Persian rule. Soon much in demand as a poet and entertainer, Anacreon did accept an invitation from Polycrates, tyrant of Samos, in 532BC. Tyrant and poet became close friends and Anacreon wrote songs celebrating love and wine. After Polycrates' capture by the Persians in 522BC, the poet moved to the court of the Pisistratid tyrants in Athens. The fall of the Pisistratids in 510BC only briefly disconcerted Anacreon. He was soon back in Athens praising the new democracy, which returned his regard. A statue to him was even erected on the Acropolis. His poetry is written in simple yet vigorous Ionic that conceals a detached ironic wit. It appealed to Romans like Horace.

SIMONIDES 556–468BC AND BACCHYLIDES 516–450BC

Poetry is seldom a family business, but Simonides managed to gain an entrée at court in Syracuse for his nephew Bacchylides. Born on Ceos, Simonides gained the patronage of Hipparchus the Pisistratid ruler of Athens. After the fall of the Pisistratids, he moved to Thessaly. He then returned to Athens to beat Aeschylus in the contest to write an epitaph on the dead after the Battle of Marathon in 490BC. A friend of Themistocles, the leading democratic politician, Simonides left Athens in 476BC as Themistocles' political power waned.

In Sicily he resolved the conflict between Hieron I, tyrant of Syracuse, and Theron, the ruler of Acragas, as a result becoming effectively Syracuse's court poet. Simonides was famed for his epigrams, especially his epitaphs, and also wrote hymns, elegies and drinking-songs. His style, always graceful, gained in power as he grew older.

Bacchylides, also a native of Ceos, first wrote poems in praise of local athletes but soon connections with Thessaly led to successes there and later on the wealthy island of Aegina. Gaining a post in Syracuse through his uncle, Bacchylides wrote odes praising Hieron's sporting victories at Olympia in 468BC.

After the death of Hieron in 467BC, Bacchylides found no other court post and had to return to Cos, where he praised his countrymen's athletic successes. His style was often compared to that of a nightingale.

Above: Pindar of Thebes (518–438BC), the greatest poet of his age, in a Roman copy of a bronze Greek original.

Below: Anacreon (with Dionysus and Eros), as pictured by Jean-Léon Gérôme in the 19th century. A versatile poet, Anacreon wrote for Sicilian tyrants as well as Athenian democrats.

PINDAR 518–438BC

Arguably the greatest poet of his age and the first notable Boeotian poet since Hesiod, Pindar came from an aristocratic family. Despite being educated in Athens and later travelling widely, Pindar remained essentially Boeotian – narrowly conservative – in outlook, devoted to his class and also to tyrants. Above all, he praised aristocrats' athletic victories, a field where they long remained supreme.

His first odes praised the Aleuad nobles of Thessaly. Soon commissions from Aegina and Sicily spread his fame, but, like many Boeotians, he faced an agonizing dilemma during the Persian invasion of 480–479BC about whether to "medize" i.e. support the Persians. How Pindar himself behaved is unclear. After the Persian defeat in 479BC, his Sicilian connections led to a welcome opening at Hieron's court in Syracuse and so to useful commissions from Syracuse and other tyrants. But Simonides and nephew were too well established at court to be dislodged, as Pindar sourly noted.

Back in Greece, Pindar's reputation as master of odes and hymns continued to grow, both in mainland cities such as Athens and Corinth and in the islands. Yet towards the end of his life, with the seemingly unstoppable rise of Athenian power and of democracy, Pindar felt increasingly out of tune with the age.

About 45 of Pindar's poems survive, nearly all odes about sporting victors. Four books of *Epinician Odes* (so-called because they were sung celebrating victories in the Games) are extant. Greatest of these is his Fourth Pythian Ode of 462BC. Very long (12 pages in translation), it contains some of his grandest poetry, full of mythical resonance and invocations, with complex, varied metres. His style has been called eagle-like, but he has also been called a scholars' poet.

Right: Many Greek poets celebrated athletes' victories in the Panhellenic games, of which the greatest were those held quadrennially at Olympia.

Whatever the judgement, Pindar had a high opinion of his calling: "Muse you have raised me up/To be your chosen messenger of fine words/To the fine dancing-places of Hellas."

Above: A fine dekadrachm (ten-drachmae coin) of Syracuse, celebrating the defeat of Carthage in 480BC, which heralded a long peace.

LATER POETS AND OTHER WRITERS c.310–80BC

Above: Roman fresco of Jason with the Golden Fleece and Medea, the subject of Apollonius' 6,000-line epic.

Below: Theocritus created the pastoral, poems about arcadian idylls in the country. His dreamy eroticism inspired Renaissance artists like Giorgione who painted Concert Champêtre *(Pastoral Concert). Titian probably completed this work after Giorgione died in 1510.*

The great literary achievements of Athens in the 5th century BC were in drama and history, with lyric poetry for a time becoming less popular. After Alexander the Great's conquests (334–323BC) over-turned the Greek world, new audiences emerged for poetry in the new cities. Their increasingly urbane citizens enjoyed witty sophisticated poems, along with romantic pastoral verse tinged with nostalgia for country life. Poets were now often also scholars in royal libraries, some-times feuding bitterly with one other. All now wrote in the *koine*, the common Greek dialect based on Attic (Ionian), the lingua franca of this wide new world.

THEOCRITUS c.310–250BC

Born in Syracuse, Theocritus' poetry was rooted in his early memories of Sicilian rustic life. The idyllic – in truth idealized – life of Sicilian shepherds figures so prominently in his verse that it is called 'pastoral'. Theocritus wrote poems to Hieron II, the new ruler of Syracuse, in 275BC but by 272BC he was writing a panegyric praising Ptolemy II king of Egypt. For the next few years Theocritus lived at the glittering Ptolemaic court at Alexandria, but he finally settled on the island of Cos. There he wrote his famous pastoral poems. These are set in imagi-nary landscapes but contain accurate observations of plant life, especially that of the eastern Aegean. Theocritus' wit spices his nostalgia in a way that was very appealing at the time and proved hugely influential on later poets from Virgil in the 1st century BC to Shakespeare and Milton in more recent times.

APOLLONIUS RHODIUS c.300–247BC

Despite his name, Apollonius was a native of Alexandria, the booming metropolis. He became at one stage head of its famous Library. He had an (almost equally) famous blazing row with Callimachus, a rival poet who insisted that epic poetry was obsolete in the new era. To prove him wrong, Apollonius wrote a huge (6,000 line) epic, *Argonautica*, about Jason and the Argonauts. Seen in its totality, this is an over-detailed antiquarian failure, but it has fascinating and beautiful passages. Apollonius was especially good at portraying romantic love from a woman's viewpoint – a rarity among Greeks, which influenced the Latin poet Ovid's love poetry nearly 300 years later.

CALLIMACHUS c.305–240BC

Born in Cyrene (today in Libya, then part of the Ptolemaic Empire), Callimachus became a leading figure among the intel-lectual elite of Alexandria in its heyday. Like many other literary men, he was a polymath. Callimachus worked in the great Library – although he was twice passed over for the post of Head Librarian – and compiled its first huge catalogue in

120 books. His other prose works include a chronology of the great dramatists, a book on the Seven Wonders of the World and many books on topics ranging from the winds to nymphs, birds and rivers. He reputedly wrote 800 slim volumes of poetry, but only fragments survive. However, as he aimed at – and often achieved – perfection on a very small scale (hence his quarrel with Apollonius), this has not harmed his reputation. His elegant wit emerges in the fragment *The Lock of Berenice* praising the Ptolemaic queen Berenice. Judging by most of his love poems, though, Callimachus was mainly attracted to boys.

PAUSANIAS C.AD120–180

Living through the Roman Empire's peaceful zenith in the 2nd century AD, Pausanias was probably the first man who can be called a travel writer. But he was far more than a mere tourist guide, being encyclopaedically knowledgeable. Born in Lydia (western Turkey), he travelled around Asia Minor, Syria, Palestine, Egypt and Greece. His ten books about Greece have survived and kept him famous.

Pausanias wrote primarily for wealthy philhellenic Romans visiting what were already ancient cities. His books combine archaeology, history, art, religion, architecture and folklore. He not only wrote lengthily and intelligently about all the major sites – Delphi, Athens, Sparta, Olympia – but also sought out, and was genuinely interested in, the most obscure places and the rituals and legends connected with them.

Although he shows little interest in natural beauty, many sites give him an excuse for a historical digression. For example, in mentioning the statues of the

Right: The statue of Zeus at Olympia, made by Pheidias in c.428BC, was so huge that, even though he was seated, the god's head brushed the temple roof. Long destroyed, it is known to us chiefly through writers like Pausanias. This 18th-century engraving by J.A. Deisenbach is wildly imaginative.

Ptolemies and Lysimachus in Athens, he launches into a detailed account of the wars of the Successors, the dynasts who carved out rival kingdoms at Alexander's death. His viewpoint is that of a patriotic Greek although he admired the emperor Hadrian. His books have proved invaluable for later historians and can be seen as forerunners of modern guide books.

Above: The palaestra (wrestling-school) of Olympia, one of the many sites vividly described by Pausanias.

A	B	Γ	Δ
Alpha	Beta	Gamma	Delta

E	Z	H	Θ
Epsilon	Zeta	Eta	Theta

I	K	Λ	M
Iota	Kappa	Lambda	Mu

N	Ξ	O	Π
Nu	Xi	Omicron	Pi

P	Σ	T	Y
Rho	Sigma	Tau	Upsilon

Φ	X	Ψ	Ω
Phi	Chi	Psi	Omega

Above: The Greek alphabet from which our present Roman (Latin) alphabet derives. The Greek alphabet had fewer letters than ours.

Below: An ostrakon *(pottery fragment) with the name of Aristides, the Athenian statesman ostracized in 482BC. Pottery supplied a cheap writing material for such actions.*

LITERACY, LIBRARIES, SCHOLARS AND SCROLLS

Around 700BC the Greeks adopted the Phoenician alphabet, adding vowel symbols to the consonant signs adequate for Phoenician. In doing so they created a simple, flexible way of writing that was to help make mass literacy possible. Our own Roman (or Latin) alphabet derives from the Greeks'. Inscriptions in Greek are widespread on monuments – on tombs, temples, walls, gateways – and as graffiti, scratched even on the statues of Abu Simbel in Egypt by Greek mercenaries. By 500BC most Greeks, at least in the major cities, were half-literate i.e. they could read if not always write.

This limitation is revealed by the story about the Athenian politician Aristides. Facing ostracism (temporary exile) by popular vote in 482BC, he was stopped by a citizen and asked to inscribe his own name on an *ostrakon* (the pottery shard used for such votes). Aristides did, so meriting his nickname the Just but also indicating that citizens could generally read if not write names. The material used shows something else: the lack of a cheap and convenient writing material. Paper, today so common, was unknown.

PAPYRUS AND PARCHMENT
In antiquity the main writing material was papyrus, which comes from the papyrus plant – our word paper derives from it – grown almost exclusively along the Nile

Above: An imaginary painting of the great Library at Alexandria in one of the frequent fires that threatened it. It survived, however, until the end of the Graeco-Roman world.

in Egypt. A tiny amount was also grown in Syracuse. Papyrus, a royal monopoly in Egypt, was expensive, but provided a fine writing material when made into scrolls.

Text was written in vertical columns, which the reader slowly unwound from one roll and wound on to another. As many texts were 8m (25ft) long, this made reading a cumbersome business, requiring two hands. Also, papyrus was fragile. For daily use, other forms of writing material were used, from *ostraka* (discarded after use) to wooden boards rubbed clean of chalked messages.

In the 2nd century BC the kings of Pergamum, great rivals of the Ptolemies of Egypt, pioneered the development of parchment, made from treated animal hides. Parchment (vellum) was tougher than papyrus, though less easy to write on. When parchment sheets began being sewn together into a *codex* (bound book)

Right: A Ptolemaic schoolboy's workbook from Egypt, made of wood and showing Greek writing. Even in the land where papyrus grew, it was too expensive for schoolboys to use.

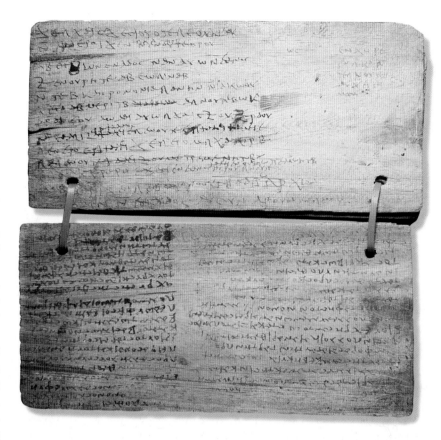

in the 3rd century AD, parchment slowly displaced papyrus. By the 6th century AD this process was almost complete.

LIBRARIES AND LIBRARIANS

Euripides, the Athenian dramatist, built up the first library in the 5th century BC. However Aristotle, the encyclopaedic philosopher, started the first proper library in the 4th century for his school, the Lyceum, in Athens. After his death in 322BC, scholarly studies moved to the richer city of Alexandria, where Ptolemy I founded the great Library in c.295BC. Attached to the Museum, which was more university than museum, the Library became the greatest in the ancient world, holding up to 600,000 scrolls. Scrolls were wrapped round sticks, identified with tags and stacked like loose rolls of wallpaper in numbered cupboards, boxes and barrels. The index alone came to 120 scrolls. Outside this "chicken coop of the muses", were cool, open colonnades beneath which scholars could work.

Many great literary or scientific men became head librarians: Apollonius of Rhodes, Eratosthenes and Aristarchus of Samothrace. The Library was concerned as much with science as the humanities.

Only slightly damaged in fighting between Julius Caesar's troops and the Alexandrians in 47BC, the Library thrived under the Romans. But the emperor Aurelian's brutal reconquest of Egypt in AD275 may have started its decline, which was accelerated by Christian attacks on Hellenic learning. By the time the Arabs captured the city in the 7th century AD, the Library had almost ceased to function.

Below: A terracotta figure found in Thebes dating from c.500BC of a man writing. By that time literacy was common among Greeks, at least in the major cities.

READING WITH MOVING LIPS?

It was once thought that the Greeks read only with their lips moving, suggesting they read with some difficulty. More recently, scholars, on re-examining ancient literary sources, have realized that many Greeks could indeed read silently. In Euripides' play *Hippolytus*, Theseus, confronted with his wife's corpse, silently reads the letter containing Phaedra's false accusation against his son Hippolytus. Then he bursts out saying that "the letter shrieks, its howls horror insufferable... a voice speaks from the letter." Plutarch related that Alexander was silently reading a confidential letter from his mother when Hephaestion "quietly put his head beside Alexander's and read the letter with him. Alexander could not bear to stop him but took off his ring and placed the seal on Hephaestion's lips", reminding his closest friend that such letters are indeed confidential. All of which suggests that at least some of the Greeks could read without moving their lips.

CHAPTER IV

PHILOSOPHY AND SCIENCE

Philosophy 'begins in wonder' – and it began with the Greeks. The Greeks were the first to think systematically, almost free of constraints, about the universe and humanity's place in it. Ethics, logic, metaphysics, philosophy itself – Greek words for concepts the Greeks originated. Western philosophy stands so firmly on Greek foundations that to call it "footnotes to Plato" (as the 20th-century philosopher A.N. Whitehead did) seems only an exaggeration. The freedom that Greek city-states gave their intellectually more daring citizens was not unlimited. There was the odd backlash against free thought, most famously in Athens with Socrates, but there was far more intellectual freedom in a polis than in any earlier (and most later) states. This freedom continued for almost 1,000 years even under Roman rule, although after 320BC many philosophers ignored politics, seeking instead inner happiness and freedom (*eudaimonia*).

Philosophical enlightenment affected the physical sciences. Early philosophers were often also scientists. Astronomy, biology, geography, maths and zoology are all Greek words. Although Socrates concentrated mostly on ethics, and Plato spurned the natural world, Aristotle was hugely knowledgeable about the natural world *and* human affairs. There were significant advances also in technology, too often under-rated. Medicine under the Greeks first became a field for rational inquiry, reaching levels unsurpassed for 1,500 years.

Left: Raphael's vision of The School of Athens *of 1510 shows Plato and Aristotle flanked by other philosophers.*

THE IONIANS: THE WORLD'S FIRST PHILOSOPHERS 600–500BC

Above: Thales (c.625–547BC), the first known philosopher and natural scientist, came from the great Ionian city of Miletus. He predicted the solar eclipse of 585BC.

Philosophy began in the small cities of Ionia on the west coast of Asia Minor around 600BC. There some men first had the freedom and audacity to ask fundamental questions about the universe. Their answers, if sometimes inaccurate, were never absurd. However most of our knowledge of them comes only through Aristotle, writing 200 years later.

THALES C.625–547BC

A native of Miletus, then the richest Greek city, Thales is considered the founder of natural philosophy. He foretold the solar eclipse of 28 May 585BC, which stopped a battle between the Lydians and Medes, both being superstitiously terrified. Such accuracy – about its exact place more than time – suggests that Thales knew of astronomy in Babylon, whose records went back centuries.

Traditionally Thales also visited Egypt to learn geometry from its priests, but his speculations about the nature of things owed nothing to priestly precedent. Observing that at low temperature water becomes like rock and at high temperature vaporizes, that land is surrounded by water and water falls from the sky, Thales deduced that water is the primary principle of everything.

He probably also regarded the Earth as spherical, a truly radical idea. Crucially, he reached his conclusions not through divine revelation or scripture but by observing and *thinking*. Although poor, Thales showed commercial acumen once by cornering the market in olive presses before a bumper harvest he had foreseen. He also urged the disparate Ionian cities to unite against the Asian empires rising in the east – in vain. He was later revered as one of the Seven Sages of Greece.

ANAXIMANDER C.610–C.540BC

A pupil of Thales, also from Miletus, Anaximander rejected his master's belief in the primacy of water. He thought instead that this world, and countless other worlds beyond our knowledge, came into being out of the *apeiron* – infinity, the basis of existence. From this have split off 'innumerable worlds'. He was the pioneer of geometrical (if mistaken) astronomy, suggesting the Earth was a huge cylinder, floating unsupported in space, equidistant from all else, and that the planets (counting the Sun and Moon as such) moved in orbits. Anaximander is also credited with making the first map and *gnomon* (sundial), of huge importance

Left: A Roman mosaic of Anaximander, the second Milesian philosopher, is credited with making the first gnomon (sundial). He also suggested theories about the evolution of animals from the sea after studying fossils.

in an age without clocks, and speculating about the evolution of living creatures from the sea after studying fossils.

His cosmological views were so radical that they were rejected by his own pupil Anaximenes, who thought the Earth was flat and the stars were fiery leaves. The cosmos consisted of air of differing densities. Anaximenes' views at the time proved more acceptable than his master's.

PYTHAGORAS c.570–c.497BC

The first man actually to be called a philosopher (lover of wisdom), Pythagoras was a philosopher/mathematician, conjuror and mystic. Born on the island of Samos, he left to escape the rule of its tyrant Polycrates. Settling at Croton in southern Italy in c.530BC, he founded a secretive community where his disciples long remained. Said to wear white robes and a gold coronet, Pythagoras declaimed (supposed) poems by Orpheus. Like the Orphics, he believed in an immortal soul that might be reincarnated as an animal. This made him a vegetarian.

Pythagoras' great mathematical discovery was that the sum of the squares on the two shorter sides of a right-angled triangle equals the sum of the square on the remaining side, the hypotenuse. He also discovered the harmony of octaves and had a mystical belief in Number, which he saw ruling the universe. Astronomy and harmony were, he said, sisters. Bertrand Russell considered him "one of the most important men that ever lived", for in him the perennial conflict in Greek thought between the rational and the mystical first surfaces. Although he left no writings, Pythagoras greatly inspired Plato.

XENOPHANES OF COLOPHON
c.570–c.480BC

Xenophanes quit his small native city after it fell to the Persians in 545BC to spend life in Sicily. He attacked Homer for his frivolous and immoral depictions of the Olympian gods, and poets for their anthropomorphic concepts of deities in general. "Thracians depict gods as

Left: Bust of Pythagoras of Samos, the first man to be called a 'philosopher', united mysticism and maths in an esoteric mixture. Reputedly he believed in reincarnation, but no writings by him survive. He and his followers settled in southern Italy.

Thracians, Africans as Africans. If horses or cattle had hands and could draw, they would create gods like horses or cattle," he claimed, a startlingly novel viewpoint that found few followers at the time. As a natural philosopher he oddly assumed that the earth was flat and the sky extended indefinitely upward. From this he concluded that each day a totally new sun rose in the east, expiring at sunset.

Below: Thales believed that the fundamental principle of the whole cosmos was water – a reasonable belief for a Greek living by the sea.

PRE-SOCRATIC PHILOSOPHERS OF THE 5TH CENTURY BC

After the defeat of the Ionian revolt against Persia in 494BC, intellectual life moved to Athens. The booming, usually liberal city for centuries attracted thinkers from around the Greek world. Those living before Socrates are called Pre-Socratic.

HERACLITUS
FLOURISHED C.500–490BC

A native of Ephesus, Heraclitus was renowned both for his personal arrogance and the obscurity of his philosophical aphorisms. About 120 of these survive. Heraclitus rejected earlier quests for a single imperishable entity beneath the constant flow of phenomena, proclaiming: *panta rei, ouden menei* (all is flux, nothing is stable). He saw the world as the unending conflict of opposites, governed by the unchanging Logos (principle, order, word). He believed that the world consisted of three cosmic elements – earth, water and fire – forever changing into each other. The greatest was fire, linked to Logos: "Fire is the underlying element, the world is everlasting fire." Although he ridiculed Xenophanes, he too believed in relativism, pointing out that the way up a mountain is also the way down. Many of his more radical aphorisms shocked contemporaries. Dead bodies, he said, smell nastier than excrement.

PARMENIDES C.510–C.430BC AND ZENO C.490–C.430BC

Parmenides, said Plato, had "magnificent depths". He is increasingly seen as the most significant Pre-Socratic, for with his thinking consciousness becomes aware of itself. This led to the human mind first recognizing its unique cognitive powers, an intellectually vital step.

Parmenides was an aristocrat from Elea, a Greek city in Italy, who visited Athens in *c.*440BC. His work survives in a three-part poem in hexameters of 150 lines. The *Prologue* is a mystic revelation by a goddess who explains two ways. *The Way of Truth*, expounded with rigorous logic, concludes by showing that all that truly exists must be one, eternal, undifferentiated and changeless. Whatever is cannot come into being or cease to exist. Conversely, that which is *not* cannot come into being. Change, therefore, is impossible. As this is clearly not the phenomenal world our senses reveal, our senses are somehow wrong. In *The Way of Opinion* he restated conventional views but only to rebut them. By confining truth to the realm of an unchanging One, Parmenides' ideas deeply influenced Plato.

Above: Raphael's portrait of the enigmatic Heraclitus, another philosopher from Miletus, who proclaimed that "all is flux".

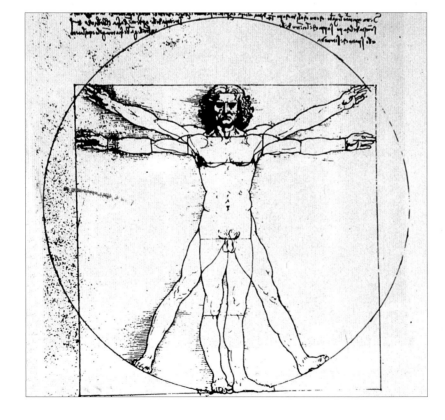

Left: Leonardo da Vinci's drawing of a perfectly symmetrical 'Vitruvian Man' illustrates Protagoras' belief that "Man is the measure of all things."

Zeno of Elea, Parmenides' main follower, defended his master's teachings against pluralist critics by extending their arguments *ad absurdum* in "Achilles' Paradox". Though Achilles runs much faster than a tortoise, if he gives the tortoise a head start in a race he will never *logically* catch up with it, because at each distinct stage the tortoise will still be an ever-reducing stage ahead.

ANAXAGORAS C.500–428BC

Born in the tiny Ionian city of Clazomenae, Anaxagoras moved to Athens in *c.*480BC. He lived there for nearly 50 years, becoming a teacher and friend of Pericles. He tried to refute Parmenides' logical monism by postulating a plurality of eternal, qualitatively different substances. His version of cosmic history began, rather like the Big Bang, when *Nous* (Mind) 'the finest and purest of all things', started a rotatory process that formed the stars and other bodies from air, separating dark from light, wet from dry. All creatures, not just humans, have minds but *Mind* is separate and infinite. Anaxagoras was nicknamed 'Mind' for stressing this but he was essentially a materialist. He was also a perceptive astronomer. He realized that the Moon shines with the Sun's reflected light and considered the Sun a "fiery rock larger than the Peloponnese." Such observations struck many Athenians as impious – the heavenly bodies were thought divine – and Anaxagoras had to retire to Lampsacus in 430BC when Pericles lost office. There he was honoured and died.

PROTAGORAS C.485–C.415BC

A native of Abdera on the Hellespont, Protagoras was probably the greatest Sophist. Sophists ('wise men') travelled around Greek cities teaching and charging fees. Protagoras taught *areté* (virtue, excellence, valour, goodness) not as an abstract virtue but as a form of life skill. Rhetoric (public eloquence) formed an important part of his training. Plato portrays him hostilely in the dialogue

Above: Athens became the centre of philosophy after the Ionian revolt was crushed by Persia in 494BC. Many Ionian thinkers found a welcome in its (usually) liberal democracy. It kept this reputation until the very end of the ancient world.

named after him, attacking his then novel concept of moral relativism, but Protagoras was widely admired. He was asked by Pericles to draw up a constitution for Thurii in Italy, and was Abdera's ambassador in Athens. In *On Truth*, one of his extant works, he famously proclaimed: "Man is the measure of all things!" Such exultant humanism led him to disregard theology. "Of the gods I know nothing, whether or not they exist nor what they are like. Many things prevent such knowledge: the obscurity of the subject, the shortness of human life." Instead, Protagoras concentrated on imparting areté in Athens at its Periclean noon.

Below: Black-figure amphora of runners. Zeno of Elea produced the argument ad absurdum *of "Achilles' Paradox". Although he runs faster, if Achilles gives the tortoise a start he can never logically catch up with it.*

Above: Greek bas-relief of Socrates talking to Diotima, the priestess sometimes called his muse, who revealed to him the potentially transcendent nature of eros (desire).

Below: The Death of Socrates, painted by J.L. David in 1787. Condemned to death for his unorthodox religious views, Socrates swallowed hemlock while debating with his disciples. He thus became a model martyr for free speech.

SOCRATES: THE ARCHETYPAL PHILOSOPHER c.470–399BC

The first Athenian-born philosopher, Socrates changed the focus of philosophy from speculation about the physical world to ethical issues. In doing so, he also became the archetypal philosopher in his disdain for worldly riches, his intellectual curiosity and his bravery. Socrates likened himself to a gadfly, stinging people into thought. Like a fly, he was finally squashed. He has often been considered an intellectual martyr. Like Christ and the Buddha, he wrote nothing, so we must rely on others' conflicting accounts of his life and thought. But the bare facts of his life are clear.

SOCRATES THE MAN

The son of a stonemason of the hoplite middle-class, Socrates fought bravely in the army, notably at Delium in 424BC. By then he was well-known enough to be ridiculed by Aristophanes in *The Clouds*, where he is portrayed as a charlatan teaching young Athenians to lie and study godless astronomy. If a travesty of the truth – although Socrates may have been interested in natural science for a time – this was an accurate enough portrait to amuse citizens.

Socrates was already attracting a circle of followers, mostly leisured young aristocrats, but anyone could listen to him debating in the Agora or street. Charging no fees, unlike the Sophists, Socrates became impoverished on abandoning his mason's trade, going around in rags. His wife Xanthippe objected to this neglect but Socrates had set his mind on higher things. This made him seem indifferent to wealth, sex and drink. The handsome young aristocrat Alcibiades tried to seduce Socrates – who was notably ugly if charming – but got nowhere, to his amazement. Equally amazing was Socrates' indifference to cold, shown on northern campaigns. He also was unaffected by alcohol, no matter how much he drank. However he was governed by his *daimon*, an inner guide that often forbade him to do things but never urged him on.

THE SOCRATIC METHOD

According to Plato's *Apology*, a prime biographical source, Socrates' intellectual quest began when the Delphic oracle declared that there was none wiser than him. Amazed, he declared himself ignorant but determined to find wise men by the Socratic method. (This is also called *elenctic*, refuting an argument by proving the contrary of its expected conclusion).

Such an approach led Socrates to question ordinary Athenians about fundamental, usually unchallenged concepts. "What is courage?" "What is justice?" "What is areté?" he asked, subjecting those who thought they knew the answers to probing inquiries that revealed their ignorance. This seldom made him loved, especially when he asked: "Who is truly fit to govern?" The answer appeared to be: no one.

But Socrates, despite a sharp-edged irony, was not playing word games. When he asked "What is justice?" he believed that, although laws might differ with different peoples, there was an underlying reality called 'justice'. Everyone could recognize it if they saw it clearly. Socrates wanted to demolish misconceptions to reveal the essence of justice, or of bravery or of areté. While he never claimed to have the final truth, he believed that no one knowingly does wrong. Wrong-doing stems from ignorance about man's real good. A man of true areté cannot be harmed by external factors such as imprisonment or death. Personal ruin comes from inner corruption.

TRIAL AND DEATH

Socrates did not seek public office but this was thrust on every Athenian at times by the city's direct democracy. In 406BC he was a member of the Council of 500 during the trial of the generals after the Battle of Arginusae, a pyrrhic victory with the generals blamed unfairly for the high losses after it. Amid demotic hysteria, the Council illegally tried and executed the generals collectively. Only Socrates protested against this injustice.

Two years later, with Athens under a fascistic junta, he showed equal courage by refusing its orders to arrest a prominent man whose wealth the junta wanted.

Democracy was restored in 403BC under a general amnesty, but memories persisted. Many recalled Socrates undermining old certainties, and that two of his ex-disciples had led the junta. Both reactionaries and democrats had reason to dislike him. In 399BC Anytus, a noted democrat, accused Socrates of "not recognizing the city's official gods and introducing new ones" and "corrupting the young" – strange charges superficially, for new gods were at times welcomed to Athens. In fact, both were ways of attacking Socrates for his views and associates. His self-defence was ironic and oddly jejune. The standard 501-strong jury found him guilty by a small majority.

He was not expected to remain for the death sentence but to go into exile. Instead, claiming he could not abandon his post, he stayed, discoursing on the immortality of the soul until his end. This came in a dose of hemlock – not a dignified death, involving convulsions and vomiting. "I owe a cock to Asclepius," were his last enigmatic words. Asclepius was the healer-god. Did Socrates mean he was freed at last from the disease of life?

Above: Socrates Snatching Alcibiades from Sexual Lures, *painted by J.-B. Regnault in 1791. In fact, Socrates failed to persuade the flamboyant aristocrat, once his star pupil, to devote himself properly to philosophy.*

Below: A Roman copy of a Greek bust of Socrates. The philosopher, although charming, was seen as shabby and ugly by contemporaries.

PLATO: THE GREATEST PHILOSOPHER? *c.*429–347BC

Above: This bust from the 4th century BC *is probably the most accurate portrait of Plato, suggesting his physical as well as intellectual strength. When young, he had been a noted wrestler.*

Plato, Socrates' most brilliant student, was arguably the greatest philosopher ever. Most of his work (*c.*500,000 words) survives, on subjects from cosmology to politics. Plato had a novelist's gift for portraying people vividly and wrote superb prose. His own views can be unclear because he usually wrote in dialogues, not verse as earlier thinkers had done, to stimulate discussion. His use of dialectic was to be very influential, in the 19th century G.F. Hegel and Karl Marx employed dialetic to great effect. Yet Plato considered all writing inferior to live debates.

Plato, although an aristocrat, rejected politics because of events early in his life: the junta of 'Thirty Tyrants' and the trial and execution under the restored democracy of his revered teacher in 399BC. Plato then left Athens, visiting Italy, where he stayed with the Pythagorean philosopher-ruler of Taranto and Sicily where he fell foul of the tyrant Dionysius I. Returning to Athens in *c.*387BC, he founded his Academy outside the city, for a select few to study philosophy.

Plato's 25 extant *dialogues*, along with several long letters, form the finest body of Greek prose ever written. Early dialogues, such as *Euthyphro* and *Crito*, and *Apology* (a rare monologue), give a vivid portrait of Socrates. They explore ethical, political and religious issues, with Socrates the genial, ironic, open-minded inquirer. In later dialogues Socrates the real person fades, as Plato's own ideas develop.

EROS HIGH AND LOW

In the *Symposium* (Banquet), the nature of eros (desire) is discussed. The comedian Aristophanes explains that, as once parts of a circular whole, we are forever seeking our divided selves. After the incursion of Alcibiades, very drunk, Socrates propounds what may be Plato's own view, relating a purported talk with Diotima, a priestess. She declared that physical sex of any type is the lowest form of eros. Higher is spiritual procreation, with souls uniting to create intellectual beauty. But eros at its highest transcends individuals, as the soul grasps the impersonal *idea* of beauty. Erotic desire is only the springboard for this ascent. (From *Symposium* comes our muddled concept of 'Platonic love'.)

THE MYTH OF THE CAVE

Central to Plato's philosophy is his Theory of Ideas (or Ideal Forms), propounded in the Myth of the Cave in *Republic*. (*Republic* also describes Plato's utopia, an austere society governed by an elite of Guardians, with poets and artists banned. While most people live lives of

Left: The myth of the prisoners chained in the cave, from which only philosophy can help them to escape. From a Flemish painting of the 16th century illustrating one of the crucial sections of Plato's Republic.

Right: Plato's Academy outside Athens, where the philosopher taught via dialectical debates. From a Roman mosaic.

unenlighted drudgery, women Guardians are men's equals – as revolutionary as the proposal to raise children communally.)

Imagine, says Plato, a row of prisoners in a cave, chained together facing inward, all unable to move. A great fire blazes behind them, separated by a parapet on which men walk carrying statues. Firelight casts the statues' shadows onto the inner wall. Prisoners, knowing only these shadows, take them for reality.

One day a prisoner, somehow escaping his shackles, turns round. He is at first blinded by the real fire. Even more over-whelming is the sunlight when he reaches the surface. Once over his shock, he is astonished by the beauty of reality. But, on returning to the cave, he cannot convince his fellow-prisoners of the real world above. *We* are those hide-bound prisoners, chained by our stupidity and desires to this world of shadows. Only through philosophy, grasping the eternal world of Ideas behind the transient sensual world, can we escape.

In *Phaedrus*, Plato related a comple-mentary myth: that of the Charioteer with two horses, a savage black animal filled with base sensual desires, and a white one, its spiritual opposite. The charioteer must master the black horse or it will drag him to ruin. Plato believed that our souls must strive to control or transcend our carnal desires.

THE PHILOSOPHER-KING

In 367BC the 62-year-old Plato sailed to Syracuse to be adviser to its new ruler, Dionysius II. He had been invited by Dion, a former Academy student and Dionysius' cousin, who said that the young tyrant was interested in philosophy. Despite misgivings, Plato could not ignore this chance to turn Greece's most powerful ruler into a 'philosopher-king' guided by virtue. But Dionysius, although he had intellectual interests, proved more inter-ested in wine and women than the tough

philosophical course grounded in maths that Plato proposed. Plato himself proved useless at court politics. Soon jealous courtiers turned the tyrant against Dion, who went into exile. Plato finally left Syracuse ignominiously. Yet he returned five years later at the pleading of Dionysius. He found that the tyrant now considered himself a philosopher. Plato was imprisoned and only managed to leave with great difficulty. Then Dion returned to Sicily and the island was engulfed in civil war. All seemed to show that politics and philosophy never mix.

Plato died in Athens working on *Laws*, his last, grimmest blueprint for an ideal society, based on Spartan models. This is truly authoritarian – even homosexuality is banned, although Plato himself was homosexual – and there is no religious or intellectual freedom at all. But Plato the man apparently could still laugh. After he died at a wedding-feast, Aristophanes' comedies were found by his bed.

Below: Plato disputing with Aristotle, his most brilliant pupil, who evolved a very different philosophy. Carved by Luca della Robbia in the 15th century.

ARISTOTLE: THE MASTER OF KNOWLEDGE 384–322 BC

Above: This bust, possibly based on an original by his contemporary Praxiteles, may portray Aristotle accurately rather than flatteringly.

Below: Aristotle contemplating a bust of Homer, from a painting by Rembrandt. Aristotle was as knowledgeable about literature as he was about the natural world.

Aristotle and Plato, the twin giants of Greek philosophy, are often seen as polar opposites, the former systematically examining this world, the latter gazing mystically upward to the next world. In fact they complement almost as much as they contradict each other. Aristotle studied for decades at Plato's Academy and his work shows Plato's influence, which he only gradually rejected or modified. Aristotle himself said: "Plato is dear to me, but dearer still is truth."

THE COURTLY OUTSIDER

Aristotle was born at Stagira, a small Ionic city in northern Greece, so he was a foreigner in Athens. His father was court physician to the Macedonian king Amyntas II, and Aristotle grew up in a strange royal court, not as a citizen of a polis. All his life he was notably well-dressed but remained always an outsider.

After his father died in 367 BC, Aristotle joined Plato's Academy in Athens, the "city hall of wisdom" in his words. He remained there for 20 years, his genius being recognized by Plato, but the Academy's increasing emphasis on maths did not suit its most brilliant student.

When, on Plato's death, his mediocre nephew Speusippus took over the Academy, Aristotle left to found a philosophical community near the Hellespont. There he fell in love with and married Phyllis (also called Pythias), niece of a local Greek ruler. In 342 BC he returned to Macedonia, the rising superpower, as tutor to Alexander, Philip II's son. Alexander, headstrong and romantic, was very unlike his tutor. However Aristotle imparted to the prince a love of Greek culture – Alexander especially liked Euripides' tragedies, although Homer was his idol – if not, it appears, his contempt for 'barbarians' (non-Greeks).

THE LYCEUM

By 335 BC Aristotle was back in Athens. There he founded his school: the Lyceum. Open to all, unlike the Academy, it had wide interests, becoming the world's first research institute, with library, museum, collections of natural objects and ultimately 2,000 students, then a huge number. Initially Aristotle taught while walking around its half-built colonnade, hence his school's traditional name: Peripatetic.

Aristotle systematically classified the natural world – botany and biology begin with his studies – from shellfish to stars. He dissected animal and human corpses, making notes and illustrations (since lost). Alexander sent his ex-tutor specimens during his world-conquest. When, after Alexander's death in 323 BC, war broke out between Athens and Macedonia, Aristotle fled to Chalcis "to prevent Athens repeating its mistake with Socrates", i.e. executing him. When he died in 322BC, he left 18 household slaves, indicating remarkable wealth for a philosopher.

THE GREAT CATEGORIZER

Aristotle was one of the most systematic thinkers known. He mapped out many still basic fields of inquiry, including biology, economics, logic, law, physics, metaphysics, politics, meteorology, ethics – probably no one else has ever *categorized* so many things as he did. Dante Alighieri, the medieval poet, called him *il maestro di color che sanno* (the master of those who know). However, Aristotle's writings survive only as dense, dry lecture notes, which restricts his wider appeal.

Unlike Plato, Aristotle accepted the material world, thinking it the only world we can investigate, but he was no crude materialist. While Plato believed that worldly objects are mere shadows of ideal forms, Aristotle asked: What *are* objects in this world? He thought that *form* is what give an object its purpose. A house is more than a jumble of building materials, necessary though they are. Similarly, Socrates was not just his physical constituents. An object's form exists within it, and could no more exist independently from it than a man's shape could exist apart from his body.

Aristotle's logically deduced views on form differed radically from Plato's mysticism. He posited four distinct but complementary Causes of form, which explains why a thing is what it is: the material, efficient, formal and final causes.

POETRY AND POLITICS

Aristotle's major works include *Poetics, Nicomachean Ethics, Politics, Rhetoric, Physics, Metaphysics* (so-called because it came *meta* [after] physics in the library).

Right: Aristotle (right) *gestures toward the ground while Plato points to the heavens, indicating the former's less idealistic philosophy. From Raphael's* School of Athens *in the Vatican, Rome.*

In *Poetics* Aristotle proclaimed poetry and tragedy superior to history because they portray noble actions that "rouse pity and fear, so achieving emotional cleansing (*catharsis*)." He posited a divine Unmoved Mover beyond the universe but was ambivalent about immortality.

In *Politics* (the last major Greek work on the topic), he wrote: "Man is by nature a political animal... Men come to the city to live, they stay to live the Good Life." Instead of the excellence/virtue (areté) sought earlier, he offered happiness (*eudaimonia*). Like Socrates, he saw virtue and happiness as connected. Happiness could be found through the Golden Mean. For example, bravery is the mean between cowardice and rashness. He was more realistic (or conservative) than Plato about his ideal society, accepting slavery and women's inferiority as natural, but still saw it as based on a medium-sized polis. While Alexander was overturning the political world, Aristotle was laying the groundwork of a logical philosophy that would dominate much of Western and Islamic thought in the Middle Ages.

Above: Aristotle being 'ridden' by his wife Phyllis. Aristotle, who had married for love, was reputedly later henpecked by Phyllis. From a drawing by Hans Baldung of c.1540.

IN SOCRATES' FOOTSTEPS
CYNICS AND SCEPTICS

Above: Diogenes, a bust of the 3rd century BC showing this most original philosopher in a sombre mood, unusual for someone normally so cheerful.

Below: Diogenes was noted for his ascetically minimalist life. Seeing a boy drinking without even a mug, he threw his away his own. From a painting by Etienne Jeurat of the 18th century.

Socrates' followers varied from the high-minded Plato to the hedonistic Aristippus of Cyrene (435–356BC). Aristippus thought undeferred pleasure the one worthwhile goal, preferably the "smooth motions of the flesh". He practised what he preached, but his school, perpetuated by his grandson, impressed few Greeks. In contrast, two other schools at odds with mainstream thinking flourished: Cynicism and Scepticism.

DIOGENES THE CYNIC C.404–325BC
Plato in irritation called Diogenes "Socrates gone mad". Certainly the great Athenian thinker inspired Diogenes, but for Diogenes life finally proved a comedy, not a tragedy.

Diogenes came from Sinope, a Greek city on the Black Sea, where his father was imprisoned for currency-forging. Diogenes, also implicated, was exiled, moving to Athens. There he became a follower of Antisthenes (*c.*445–360BC),

once a student of Socrates. Antisthenes dressed like a poor labourer, rejecting public affairs, private property, marriage and established religion. (That he could spurn religion publicly shows that Athens, after Socrates' trial, had regained its normal tolerance.) Antisthenes generally discouraged followers but Diogenes was his most persistent disciple, who would not be dissuaded even by a stick. With Diogenes the Cynics became a school – if dropouts can be said to form a school.

LIVING LIKE DOGS
Cynic (*cynicos*), meaning dog-like, was an insult happily accepted by Diogenes. He flouted social customs in an ultra-Socratic quest for truth and virtue, but was not remotely 'cynical' in today's negative sense. Once asked why he was carrying a lantern in daylight, he replied that he was looking for an "honest man".

Diogenes had no house but lived in a barrel. He had one ragged cloak for the day that was his blanket at night. He begged for his food, having one bowl and one mug. But when he saw a boy drinking from his cupped hands, he threw away even his mug as superfluous.

Diogenes satisfied all his bodily functions in public, even masturbating. When rebuked for this – the Greeks admired heroic nudity, not sexual exhibitionism – he simply said: "Ah, if only I could satisfy my hunger by rubbing my belly."

Effectively stateless, having no polis, he claimed to be a *cosmopolitan*, a "citizen of the universe". Captured by pirates and put up for sale as a slave, Diogenes was asked if he had any special skills. "Governing men," he replied, and pointed to a well-dressed man. "Sell me to him, he needs a master." He was freed by friends. Finally dying from eating raw octopus – to show that cooking is unnecessary – he ordered his corpse thrown in a ditch.

Ignoring these last wishes – which outraged the deepest religious beliefs – Athens erected a marble monument with a dog to this most original of thinkers.

Diogenes' aim was not to win fame by crude sensationalism but to show that almost all material wants can be discarded. Like many later philosophers, he sought not areté (virtue) but eudmamonia (happiness) and ataraxia (freedom from worry or care). His successor Crates of Thebes (c.365–285BC) renounced great wealth to live a similar wandering life. Crates' wife Hipparchia, who was famous for her beauty, was among the few noted female philosophers. Cynicism survived under the Roman Empire. It in some ways anticipated the Stoics, Christian ascetics and even, much later, the hippies.

PYRRHO THE SCEPTIC c.365–275BC

Among the Greeks who followed Alexander to India was Pyrrho of Elis. He was so impressed by the diversity of customs and beliefs that he saw, especially among Indian fakirs, that he became the founder of scepticism. He argued that the reasons for a belief are never better than those against, and that the only wise approach is to suspend judgement and accept the world as it seems. His goal was ataraxia, like Diogenes. Pyrrho often pointed to animals as living enviably undisturbed lifes. He retired to Elis, where he lived out a long and peaceful life amid admirers.

Pyrrho's chief pupil, Timon of Phlius, (c.320–230BC) took scepticism further, showing that every argument proceeds from premises not already established. To demonstrate those premises' truth by other arguments, they must be based on other undemonstrated premises, a potentially infinite and so absurd regression.

Timon's follower Arcesilaus (315–240BC) became head of Plato's Academy in 275BC, making it a bastion of scepticism for about 200 years. Timon's successor Carneades caused a stir when visiting Rome by arguing both sides of a cause on successive days. Cicero was later influenced by the Academy's scepticism. The best account of scepticism comes from Sextus Empiricus' summary of its arguments in the *Pyrrhoniarum* of c.AD200. David Hume, the great 18th-century Scottish philosopher, was inspired by Pyrrhonic scepticism.

Above: Bion of Olbia (c.325–255BC) was an eclectic philosopher, intellectually closest to the Cynics. He lived by wandering around the major cities teaching, but finally gained the patronage of Antigonus II, king of Macedonia.

Left: Alexander the Great and the barrel-dwelling Diogenes reputedly met in Corinth in 335BC. When Alexander asked what he could do for the thinker, Diogenes replied: "Get out of my sunlight."

RIVAL SCHOOLS
STOICS V. EPICUREANS

Above: A copy of an original statue of c.240BC of Chrysippus, the second great Stoic teacher, who emphasized ethics over logic and physics in a way that proved very appealing.

Two rival schools of thought, Stoicism and Epicureanism, emerged around 300BC in Athens to become the main forms of philosophy for centuries.

STOICISM
Stoicism was founded by Zeno of Citium (333–262BC). Zeno, reaching Athens in 311BC, attended the Academy, listened to Crates the Cynic and studied Aristotle before evolving his own philosophy. He taught in the Stoa Poikile (Painted Stoa) from which his school takes its name. His courses were tripartite: logic, physics and ethics. His teachings were refined by his successors Cleanthes and Chrysippus (c.280–207BC). Chrysippus downplayed logic and physics in favour of ethics, creating an appealing philosophical package.

The essence of Stoicism was that nothing happens by chance, all things being predetermined by the laws of the cosmos. There is nothing higher than the natural universe, of which we are part. We must live in harmony with it, accepting everything that happens. Stoics proclaimed a "brotherhood of man" that included slaves and non-Greeks. Although they raised a god (called Zeus) to quasi-pantheistic primacy, they did not believe in individual afterlife. Nor did they forbid suicide.

Left: The stern nobility of Epicurus is apparent in this bust. Far from advocating sensual indulgence, as his enemies said, Epicurus thought most pleasures were not worth the effort. He abjured politics, fame and – guardedly – any real belief in the gods, valuing friendship above everything.

Poseidonius (c.135–51BC), a polymathic Stoic, travelled widely before establishing his school at Rhodes, where important Romans, including Pompey and Cicero, visited him. Cicero later translated Greek philosophical ideas into Latin and Stoicism became the favoured philosophy of the Roman elite, who found its noble austerity appealing.

ROMAN STOICS
Seneca (2BC–AD65) was a playwright and courtier, the emperor Nero's tutor and then minister. Retiring from the increasingly paranoid emperor's court, Seneca turned again to philosophy until, implicated in a conspiracy against Nero in AD65, he committed suicide. He wrote (in Latin) essays, plays and 124 letters on varied subjects, especially the humane treatment of slaves. "Remember, the man you call your slave is of the same species and breathes, lives and dies under the same skies as you." His work, if unoriginal, inspired many later generations unable to read Greek.

Epictetus (AD55–135) also suffered from imperial paranoia, being among the philosophers exiled by the emperor Domitian in AD89. He accepted this as calmly as earlier maltreatment while a slave, settling in western Greece. There he taught an austere yet compassionate philosophy, attacking easy cures for human misery that ignored the "wisdom of God". Epictetus wrote in Greek.

So did the emperor Marcus Aurelius (reigned AD161–80). Antiquity's one philosopher-king. Marcus was brought up to rule as a sage but in practice had to spend much of his reign fighting invading barbarians on the Danube frontier. His *Meditations*, written on campaign, are the private records of an exhausted if great-souled man. Tinged with Platonism, they were the last true Stoic writings.

Right: An original – and very rare – bronze statue of Marcus Aurelius, the philosopher-emperor (reigned AD161–80). The last great Stoic, he wrote his Meditations *while campaigning on the Danube. They were not meant for publication.*

EPICUREANISM

Although Epicureanism was often damned by its enemies as encouraging gross sensuality, this was a travesty of the real aims of its founder Epicurus (341–270BC). The son of Athenian colonists on Samos, Epicurus settled in Athens in 307BC. He established his Garden – literally, it was a vegetable garden – near Plato's Academy, but with very different aims: to seek human happiness, not mystical truth.

Epicurus believed the chief causes of human misery were fear of what happens after death and frustrated desires for the superfluous while alive.

He set out to demolish fear of death by showing that the soul, like the rest of the universe, is composed of constituent atoms, which simply dissolve at death. Here he was echoing the thinking of Democritus (*c*.460–370BC), an earlier atomist. There is nothing to be feared or expected after death.

Contentment in this life is best achieved by intelligent frugality, Epicurus' extant maxims suggest. "Value frugality not for asceticism's sake but because it minimizes worries… It is better to sleep without fear on a straw mattress than trembling on a gold bed … No pleasure is bad in itself but certain pleasures incur drawbacks far greater than the pleasure gained."

Epicurus shunned public life, seeing in the polis only a source of strife – an understandable reaction to the turmoil of his age, if one that marked the withdrawal of philosophers from society. Instead, he valued friendship above everything else. Never marrying, he made his Garden a refuge for the like-minded, be they citizens, slaves or women. Admitting slaves and women to his school – something Plato had only contemplated – caused a

scandal even greater than denying the afterlife. (Epicurus tactfully accepted the gods' existence but denied they were at all interested in humanity.) The Garden, emulating the Academy and Lyceum, had a communal life, with regular debates and monthly *symposia.* Often ill in later years, Epicurus lived mostly off bread and cheese and died in great pain with cheerful, indeed Stoical, fortitude.

Epicurus wrote more than 300 books on philosophy but none has survived. While his teaching proved popular in the Greek world, his greatest disciple was the Roman Lucretius (94–55BC). In *De Rerum Natura* (*About the Nature of Things*), Lucretius wrote a brilliant philosophical poem. Although Lucretius called his poetry just "honey round the edges" of his beliefs, Cicero was much impressed by this philosophy expounded so lyrically.

Below: Zeno of Citium, who settled in Athens in 311BC and founded the Stoic school of philosophy. This stresed acceptance of the universe as reflecting the divine will.

THE PLATONIST REVIVAL
PLOTINUS AND NEOPLATONISTS

Above: The spiritual nobility of Plotinus, the ancient world's last great original thinker who founded the Neoplatonist school, shines through this bust of the 3rd century AD. This might well be a portrait from life.

The last great philosophical school of antiquity was Neoplatonism. Its founder was Plotinus (*c.*AD204–70), an Egyptian Greek. Plotinus saw himself not as founding a new school but as reviving true Platonism. However, he gave Plato's thinking a deeply mystical, overwhelmingly monistic turn by positing a superexistent *One* as the source of all being, far beyond sensory perception.

Plotinus first studied under Ammonius Saccas, an obscure figure who wrote nothing. He then joined the Persian expedition of the emperor Gordian III in AD243, apparently hoping to learn about eastern religions in India. After Gordian's murder by his troops, Plotinus moved to Rome. There he started his own school.

Among his aristocratic students was Gallienus, who became emperor in AD253. Gallienus so admired Plotinus that he offered to found Platonopolis, a city for philosophers in Campania, but court intrigues aborted this utopian project. After Gallienus' death in AD268, Plotinus withdrew from public life. He had never been a worldly man. Plato, while spurning Athenian democracy, had remained interested in politics. By contrast, Neoplatonists ignored the world falling into ruin about them. Instead, they turned to the mystical *Monos* (the One).

FLIGHT OF THE ONE TO THE ONE
Porphyry (AD232–305), Plotinus' biographer and most important follower, recorded the last words of his teacher as: "Strive to bring back the god within yourselves to the God in the Universe." This

Left: Julian, the last significant non-Christian Roman emperor (reigned AD361–3), was also a Neoplatonist philosopher. His attempts to revive Hellenism as an organized religion died with him, but Greek philosophy itself survived for a time.

injunction lies at the heart of Plotinus' philosophy, simultaneously rational and mystical. His thinking incorporated Pre-Socratic, Aristotelian and Stoic ideas, creating a novel, moving philosophy.

Plotinus saw the One as the supernatural, ineffable basis of all being, resembling Plato's idea of the Good. Below this ineffable summit are tiers of being. The first is *Nous*, or Mind, the second *Psyche*, or Soul, a projection of Mind. Soul looks up to Mind but down to Nature (*Bios*), but the tiers are interdependent. Even at the lowest corporeal level, all things seek *epistrophe*, a return to the One. Plotinus' dynamic vision has been compared to an inexhaustible fountain of light whose waters constantly descend before returning to the source. He believed human beings can, via philosophy, attain ecstatic visions of the One as *fuge monou pros monon*, the "Flight of the One to the One". He claimed to have achieved this three times.

As a man, Plotinus was self-effacing and ascetic, so ashamed of bodily functions he did not even like to be seen eating. He never married, eschewing sex, but freely admitted women to his classes. These could be tortured sessions, the philosopher falling silent in his attempt to express the inexpressible. He wrote little and then only in his last years.

THE FOLLOWERS
Porphyry, born in Tyre, came to Rome in *c.*AD262 and joined Plotinus' classes. Soon the master's favourite, he recorded Plotinus' teaching in nine books, *Enneads* (*Ninths*). Like his master, Porphyry rejected Christianity because of its belief in a personal god and salvation by faith – the One is not a person, superficial resemblances to the Christian Trinity are accidental. Porphyry amended Plotinus' thought by positing the importance of

astrology. Plotinus, however, to whom the stars shone with the universe's divinity, always rejected astrology's basic premises.

Porphyry's successor Iamblichus (c.AD250–326) added *theurgy*, magical rites derived from Neopythagoreanism – more a religion than philosophy – to Neoplatonism. His synthesis shaped Neoplatonism as it spread around the Roman Empire. Schools sprang up at Alexandria, Pergamum and Athens. The last pagan emperor Julian studied this semi-magical philosophy at Athens and Pergamum. During his brief reign (AD361–3), Julian tried to revitalize paganism along Neoplatonist lines.

THE END OF GREEK PHILOSOPHY

In Alexandria one of the last Hellenic philosophers was a woman, Hypatia (c.AD370–420). A fine mathematician as well as a Neoplatonist, beautiful but celibate, Hypatia devoted her life to philosophy until one day she was dragged from her coach and murdered by a fanatical Christian mob. Despite her murder, Neoplatonism lingered on in Alexandria, but its last bastion was, appositely, Athens. There, Proclus (AD410–85) fused mathematics and mysticism to expound the interconnectedness of all things, arguing that time itself is a circular dance. Finally in AD529 the Byzantine emperor Justinian ordered the closure of the schools of Athens.

This marked the end of ancient Neoplatonism, but it had deeply influenced St Augustine (AD354–430), among the greatest Christian thinkers. Other early Christian writers, from the Roman patrician Boethius in the 6th century and Dionysus the Aeropagite (suposedly an Athenian converted by St Paul in the 1st century AD but actually a Greek

Right: Percy Bysshe Shelley (1792–1822) was one of many Romantic poets influenced by Neoplatonism, most notably in Adonais. *Here he sits writing amid the ruins of the Baths of Caracalla, Rome. From a posthumous painting by Joseph Severn.*

Right: Hypatia of Alexandria, one of the few women philosophers in Hellenic tradition, was traditionally very beautiful but celibate. A mathematician as well as a mystic, she was murdered by a mob of fanatical Christians in C.AD *420.*

contemporary of Boethius) to Eriugena in the 9th century, were also profoundly affected by Neoplatonism. (How far the last two thinkers are really Christians, rather than mystical pantheists, remains debated.)

In Renaissance Italy, Neoplatonism re-emerged fully, first inspired by Greek thinkers fleeing the fall of Constantinople to the Turks. Marsilio Ficino translated the *Enneads* while Pico della Mirandola tried to reconcile Christianity, Platonism, Judaism and even Chaldean paganism in a mystical synthesis. His heroic efforts landed him briefly in a papal prison, but Neoplatonism spread north to England. Reviving again with the Romantics, its perennial philosophy underlies much of the poetry of S.T. Coleridge, P.B. Shelley, Ralph Waldo Emerson and W.B. Yeats.

THE FIRST MATHEMATICIANS
600BC–AD200

Above: Thales, visiting Egypt in the 6th century BC, was asked by the pharaoh to calculate the height of a pyramid. He waited for the time when his shadow equalled his own height and thus calculated the height of the pyramid itself.

Below: A monument built in Samos in 1989 to Pythagoras. The mystical mathematician, born in Samos, traditionally discovered the theorem that bears his name.

Mathematics as a proper discipline began with the Greeks in the 6th century BC. The Egyptians had long been brilliant at practical calculation and measuring and the Babylonians had first divided the circle into 360 degrees, but neither had developed a series of theories based on definitions with axioms and proofs. It took Greek intellectual passion and precision to do this. Maths became so central to Greek thinking that Plato stipulated that only the numerate should enter his Academy. But Greek maths had its limits. For example, it had no term for – or concept of – zero, unlike Indian maths.

EARLY MATHEMATICIANS
Thales is considered the first Greek mathematician. Visiting Egypt in the 6th century BC, Thales was reputedly asked by the pharaoh to calculate the height of a pyramid. He waited for a time when his shadow equalled his own height and then calculated the pyramid's height. He also worked out how to calculate a ship's distance from the shore. Around 520BC, Pythagoras traditionally discovered the theorem that bears his name: that in a right-angled triangle the square of the sum of the opposite side equals the squares of the other two sides. Pythagoreans also knew that the sum of all three angles of a triangle equals two right angles. They had a mystical belief in number, being the true (if secret) unity behind the universe, manifested in musical octaves. But their discovery of incommensurability – that some ratios could not be expressed as whole numbers, a seemingly insoluble problem already encountered in Babylon – led them to concentrate on geometry.

Eudoxus of Cnidus (*c.*408–347BC) studied with the Pythagoreans at Taranto and also in Egypt. In geometry he discovered the general theory of proportions

Above: Euclid (c.330–270BC), the greatest mathematician before the late 19th century. From a portrait by the Renaissance artist Girolamo Mocetto.

applicable to both incommensurable and commensurable magnitudes, later shown by Euclid in Book 5. He also showed by the "method of exhaustion" that the cone and pyramid are one third the volume respectively of the cylinder and prism with the same base and height.

EUCLID THE MATHEMATICAL MASTER
The greatest Greek mathematician was Euclid (*c.*330–270BC), who taught at the Museum/Library of Alexandria. His famous work is his *Elements* (*Stoichea*) in 13 books. The most influential book in mathematical history, it formed the basis of

Western maths until the late 19th century. Although not all the contents are original – Plato in *Timaeus* had anticipated the treatment of regular geometric solids – Euclid added a new logical structure of such elegant clarity that Bertrand Russell called *Elements* "the most perfect monument of Greek intellect". By deducing the geometrical objects' properties from a few axioms, Euclid in effect founded the axiomatic method of mathematics. Book 1 begins with definitions followed by the famous 5 postulates. Euclid then gives a list of common notions. The first definitions are:

1.1. *A point is that which has no part.*
1.2. *A line is a breadthless length.*
1.3. *The extremities of lines are points.*
1.4. *A straight line lies equally with respect to the points on itself.*

The common notions are axioms such as: "*Things equal to the same thing are also equal to one another.*"

LATER MATHS AND ARCHIMEDES

Archimedes (287–212BC) was a brilliant mathematician as well as famed inventor. His achievements in maths were prodigious, as a list of even his surviving works suggests: *On the Sphere and the Cylinder; On the Measurement of the Circle; On Conoids and Spheroids; On Spirals; On the Equilibrium of Surfaces* where the theory of the lever is propounded, enabling him to boast "Give me somewhere to stand and I will move the Earth!"; *On the Quadratura of the Parabola* and *The Sand Reckoner*. This last work deals with the problem of expressing huge numbers. It demonstrates that the number of grains of sand in the universe, far from being infinite, may on some asumptions be reckoned as 10^{63}.

Archimedes also calculated a far closer value for Pi. He designed his own tomb incorporating a sphere inside a cylinder, to record his discovery that the sphere occupies two-thirds of the space. His most famous discovery, 'Archimedes' principle', states that a body immersed in fluid loses weight equal to the weight of

Above: Reconstruction of the lighthouse at Alexandria. At c.115m (383ft) *tall, its light both guided shipping and symbolized the city's intellectual brilliance.*

Below: Archimedes, the great mathematician of the 3rd century BC, *portrayed by José de Ribera (1591–1652).*

the amount of fluid it displaces. Archimedes traditionally realized this on stepping into his bath, crying out "Eureka" (I have found it!).

Only two of 12 works attributed to Apollonius of Perge (*c.*260–190BC), the 'Great Geometer', survive. In *Conics*, he pioneered terms such as ellipse, parabola, and hyperbola describing various types of orbit. *Conics* distilled 200 years of earlier thinking. It remained canonical even for 17th-century revolutionaries such as Descartes, Fermat and Newton.

Later Greek maths continued to develop but less vigorously. Ptolemy summarized much of it in the 2nd century AD. Diophantus (*c.*AD200–80) was the one noted Greek contributor to algebra, although only six of his works survive. He influenced the Arabs, who later proved far more original at algebra.

ASTRONOMY
MAPPING THE COSMOS 600BC–AD150

Above: Ptolemy (Claudius Ptolemaeus), the last great Hellenic astronomer, who worked in Alexandria in the 2nd century AD. From a portrait by Pedro Berruguette and Justus of Ghent c.1475.

Below: The constellation of Hercules with Corona and Lycra, from Atlas Coelestis of 1729 by John Flamsteed, painted by James Thornhill. Viewing the cosmos scientifically and mythologically is one of the Greeks' lasting achievements.

The Greeks were not the world's first astronomers. Egyptians and Babylonians had compiled detailed star charts to predict eclipses, but their knowledge remained tied to their religions. Soon after 600BC, the Greeks began to observe and speculate boldly and rationally. Thales probably used Babylonian records to predict the solar eclipse of 585BC. But his other astronomical feat, suggesting the Earth was spherical, was unprecedented. Inspired by him, Anaximander pioneered geometrical astronomy. He posited that the Sun, stars and Moon are rings of fire, respectively 27, 18 and 9 times the Earth's diameter, encased in tubes. Through holes in these tubes their light is seen. His concept of the Earth floating in space was too radical for his first successors, who reverted to cosier ideas.

CLASSICAL ASTRONOMY
In Periclean Athens (*c.*460–430BC), Anaxagoras daringly posited that the sun was a fiery stone "larger than the Peloponnese", the moon shining with its reflected light. (These were such novel ideas that Anaxagoras left Athens to escape impiety charges. These were really political, aimed at Pericles his patron.)

Pythagoreans living in Italy went much further. Restating Thales' idea of a spherical Earth, they suggested that the Earth itself is one of the planets, not the centre of the universe. All planets, including the Sun, move around the "central fire" whose light, in Pythagorean cosmogony, the Sun only reflects. The Pythagoreans also first realized that the morning and evening stars are the same planet: Venus.

Aristotle in the 4th century BC put the Earth solidly back at the centre of things, with the planets circling it. But he was an unoriginal astronomer, just restating the views of Eudoxus of Cnidus. Eudoxus had posited homocentric orbits for the planets to explain their *retrograde motions* (when seen from Earth, planets can appear to move backward). Around 330BC Callipus elaborated this system, adding further spheres for the lunar and solar orbits and calculating the year accurately at 365.25 days. Heraclides Ponticus (*c.*390–310BC) reputedly suggested that Mercury and Venus rotate around the Sun, which itself circles the Earth, pointing towards the heliocentric theory.

ARISTARCHUS' REVOLUTION
At Alexandria, whose new Library/ Mausoleum attracted Greece's brightest minds, Greek astronomy reached its climax. Its boldest thinker was Aristarchus of Samos (*c.*310–230BC). He posited the full heliocentric theory: that the Earth and other planets revolve around the Sun, the Earth itself turning every 24 hours on its own axis. To avoid the parallax (apparent movement) of the fixed stars, he placed them unimaginably far off. This solved all problems of retrograde motions. It proved too radical, however, for Aristarchus

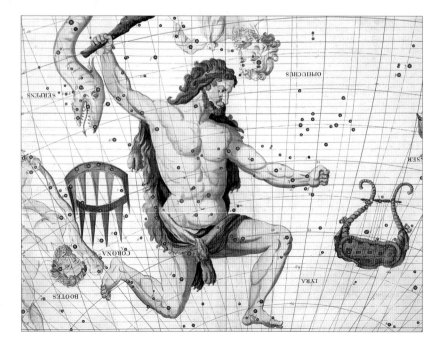

Right: The geocentric universe as envisaged by Ptolemy, with 27 concentric circles describing the orbits of the heavenly bodies from the Moon to Saturn, the farthest planet visible to the naked eye.

united other scientists against him, one trying to indict him for impiety in uprooting the Earth. Archimedes also rejected Aristarchus' ideas – without calling for his trial. Aristarchus had just one Greek follower, Seleucus, his ideas lying dormant until Copernicus in the 16th century.

THE ALEXANDRIAN ACHIEVEMENT
While sticking to the geocentric theory, Alexandria's astronomers made impressive contributions to science. Most were polymaths, such as Eratosthenes of Cyrene (275–194BC), who became Librarian in 235BC. He is renowned for calculating the Earth's diameter. Eratosthenes knew that on 21 June at noon in Syene on the Tropic of Cancer the Sun would be at its zenith. He also knew that in Alexandria the angle of the Sun's elevation would then be 7.2 degrees south of the zenith. He calculated the distance from Alexandria to Syene as 7.2/360 of the total circumference of the Earth. The distance between the cities was a known 800km (500 miles), so he worked out the Earth's circumference as 39,690km (24,663 miles), within 98% of the real figure. Like other Greek astronomers, he relied wholly on observations made by the naked eye, as they had no lenses.

Hipparchus of Nicaea (*c.*190–126BC) was probably the greatest Alexandrian astronomer. He discovered the precession of the equinoxes; estimated the length of the lunar month and catalogued 850 fixed stars, giving their longitude and latitude, and improved the theory of epicycles invented by Apollonius *c.*220BC. He based his theories both on observation and on tables going back to Babylonian records. He also noted a *nova* (new star).

Most of Hipparchus' work survives only in the *Almagest* of Ptolemy, the last Greek astronomer, living in Alexandria in the 2nd century AD. Ptolemy perfected the geocentric theory of the universe, providing detailed mathematical theories supported by observations. His belief that the same divine harmony resonated in the stars and the human soul passed to the medieval and Renaissance worlds.

Below: Syene (Aswan) in Egypt. Eratosthenes calculated the distance from Alexandria to Syene as 7.2/360 of the Earth's circumference, so giving him a remarkably accurate figure for it.

GEOGRAPHY
MAPPING THE EARTH C.550BC–AD170

Above: The Stoa at Miletus, the wealthy Ionian city where Hecataeus drew up the first known map of the world in the 6th century BC.

Below: Ptolemy of Alexandria's map of the Middle East, from Phoenicia (Lebanon) across to Babylonia (southern Iraq), drawn up in the 2nd century AD. His maps are both beautiful and functional.

The Greeks were the first geographers in the full meaning of the word. Their researches were linked to astronomers' theoretical findings – which led to the idea of the Earth as spherical – and to reports from navigators and other travellers. Greek geographical knowledge continued growing under the Romans.

THE FIRST GEOGRAPHERS (C.550–420BC)

The first geographers were also historians – *historia* meant originally any inquiry or research. Hecataeus (*c*.560–490BC), born in Miletus, travelled widely around the Mediterranean, possibly venturing into the Atlantic. He was involved in the abortive Ionian Revolt against Persia of 499–494BC, despite initially opposing it because hostile to its leader Aristagoras.

Hecataeus' great work was a map of the whole world, possibly inspired by an earlier map by Anaximander. He saw the Earth as a disc surrounded by the all-encircling Ocean, divided into four

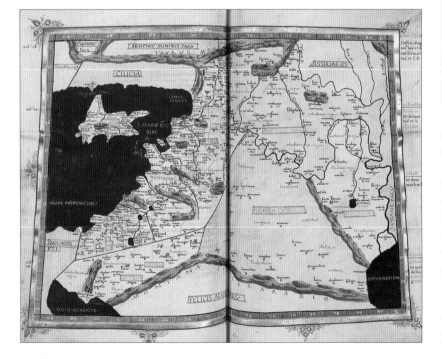

quadrants, east–west by the Mediterranean, and north–south by the rivers Ister (Danube) and Nile. Europe filled the northern half and Africa/Asia the southern half. If ridiculed for inaccuracies by Herodotus (*c*.484–420BC), his better-informed successor, Hecataeus' map was the first to state accurately the continents' relative positions.

In *Periegasis*, Hecataeus described many countries' customs, religions, fauna and flora. (In Egypt, he boasted to a priest that his ancestry went back 16 generations.

The priest replied that his own went back 345!) Hecataeus' map influenced many later generations' worldview. Herodotus, although fascinatingly informative about much of Asia and Europe, was not a cartographer.

Aristotle realized that the Earth was a globe, dividing it into zones, and his pupil Dicecarchus made a new map incorporating his changes. Otherwise geography had advanced little by the mid-4th century BC. Aristotle was uncertain whether the Caspian Sea opened on to the Ocean that Greeks thought encircled the Earth, and he confused the Caucasus with the Himalayan mountains. All changed radically with the philosopher's other pupil.

AFTER ALEXANDER

Alexander the Great's conquests (334–323BC) opened up a vast new world. Alexander himself reached the Punjab in northern India, and the voyage by his admiral Nearchus from the mouth of the Indus to the head of the Persian Gulf provided a flood of new information for geographers. This was collected and analysed at Alexandria's great Library/ Museum. Eratosthenes in the 3rd century BC worked out not only the Earth's

Below: Herodotus the great historian was also an intrepid traveller.

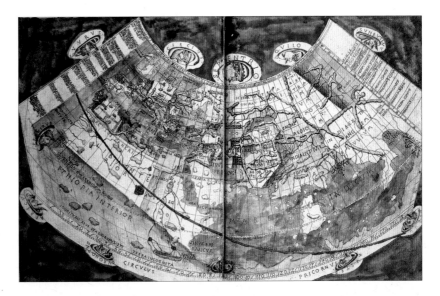

circumference but also longitudes and latitudes for many places – suggesting that he deserved more than his nickname of Beta, or second best. Hipparchus in the 2nd century BC and Posidonius in the 1st continued this work.

GRAECO-ROMAN GEOGRAPHY

Under the long *pax Romana* (Roman peace) after 30BC, geography remained primarily a Greek affair. Strabo (64BC–AD21), who came from the Greek city of Amasia on the Black Sea, travelled widely and wrote 17 books on geography. He held the view that the Earth was a sphere with all the continents, Europe, Asia and Africa, forming a single mass surrounded by the Ocean. Although Strabo claimed to have travelled as far as Ethiopia, his knowledge derives in fact mostly from Eratosthenes, whose works he thus helped to preserve.

The last great Hellenic geographer was Ptolemy of Alexandria. In the mid-2nd century AD he wrote his *Geography* in eight books. By then Rome's invasion of the British Isles, expeditions into the North Sea and trade links with India had vastly extended geographical knowledge. The map Ptolemy drew up reflected this, showing India and even, hazily, China. But he still imagined the three (known) continents as encircled by one ocean. His map remained canonical until 1492.

Above: The Earth as mapped by Ptolemy of Alexandria, who was a great cartographer as well as astronomer. Showing the three known continents, with even China hazily recognized, his ideas remained canonical until the discovery of America in 1492.

Below: Alexander's conquests led to a vast widening of Greek geographical knowledge. From an Indian Mughal painting of the 16th century.

TECHNOLOGY
THE FORGOTTEN ACHIEVEMENTS

Above: Archimedes, the most polymathic of Greek geniuses, inadvertently killed by a Roman soldier in the fall of Syracuse in 212BC. From a Roman mosaic.

Below: Found in the sea near Antikythera, dating to c.80BC, this complex bronze mechanism has 31 gear wheels. It was probably both an astronomical and a navigational device.

The Greeks were once thought to have neglected technology because they had no wish to dirty their hands with science's practical applications. Maintained by their myriad slaves, the argument ran, the Greeks saw science as a gentlemanly pursuit of no practical value. Plutarch, the 2nd-century AD historian, has been quoted to support this view: "Thinking mechanics and all utilitarian arts fit only for vulgar craftsmen, he [Archimedes] concentrated only on things where the beautiful and are not mixed with the necessary." No or little machinery meant little economic advance, and ultimately Graeco-Roman civilization's failure.

Plutarch's view is now seen as misleading, reflecting only the prejudices of his class. (Similar sentiments were frequently voiced by British aristocrats during Britain's Industrial Revolution.) If the Greeks could not match even medieval and early modern Europe's technological achievements, let alone

> ### THE ANTIKYTHERA MECHANISM
> A discovery from beneath the sea near the island of Antikythera has revealed Greek technological sophistication. Dating from c.80BC, this remarkable bronze mechanism has at least 31 gear wheels, making it a rival of any such mechanism, in Asia or Europe, before the 19th century. With orbits for the Sun, Venus and other planets, it was probably intended both as a clock and as an astronomical device, incorporating discoveries made in the Hellenistic period. It is the sophisticated ancestor of both computers and clocks, therefore. Although the only such device known today, it is unlikely to have been the only one made. Most bronze objects have been lost, however, melted down for their metal content in the Dark Ages, be they computers or clocks.

China's massive inventiveness, they made many useful inventions. Only the ancient world's political and economic limitations, and its general decline after c.AD200, precluded further technological advances by still creative polymaths. That the word *machine* comes from Greek *mekhane* is no coincidence.

One of the earliest known applications of machinery was in the theatre. Here large cranes lifted scenery and actors, usually representing gods (but once Socrates) on and off stage. These cranes, described by Aristotle, must have used a weight and pulley principle of some complexity but no remains have been found.

Similar machinery was probably used to build many of the great Greek temples, including the Parthenon in Athens, where massive blocks of marble had to be lifted high into place.

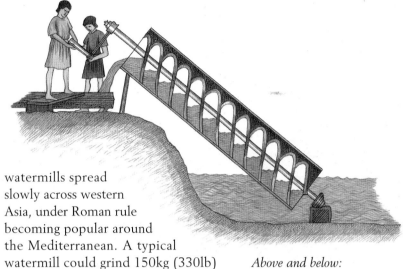

Above: The waterwheels of Bihiyat on the Orontes River. Known to the Greeks by the 4th century BC, *watermills spread in the Hellenistic and Roman periods. A watermill can grind 150kg (330lb) of grain per hour, compared to 7kg (15lb) ground by a slave.*

ARCHIMEDES' SCREW

A mathematician, astronomer and inventor of genius, Archimedes (287–212BC) was born in Syracuse. He worked in Alexandria before returning to become Hieron II's chief scientist. He devised for the powerful Syracusan king many military devices, including formidable walls, cranes that could pull ships from the sea and possibly solar mirrors to burn ships, besides a planetarium and star globe. Archimedes was killed accidentally by a Roman soldier in the capture of Syracuse, but the Romans took over his devices. He is deservedly best known for a utilitarian invention, his screw that helps irrigation.

Archimedes' Screw consists of a screw inside a hollow pipe. The lower end is put in water and the screw then turned, usually by manual labour. As the bottom of the tube turns, it scoops up water. This water slides up a spiral tube as the shaft is turned, until it finally pours out from the top of the tube to feed the irrigation systems. A cruder screw may have been used earlier by the Babylonians to water their Hanging Gardens, but Archimedes definitely developed the screw as used since.

An important labour-saving development that the Greeks adopted was the watermill. Known by the 4th century BC,

watermills spread slowly across western Asia, under Roman rule becoming popular around the Mediterranean. A typical watermill could grind 150kg (330lb) of grain per hour, compared to only 7kg (15lb) by a slave.

HERON OF ALEXANDRIA

A mathematician and engineer, Heron, who lived in Alexandria in the mid-1st century AD, was another remarkable polymath. He listed more than 80 different devices in his numerous books, mainly about hydraulics, pneumatics and mechanics. Among them are drinking fountains, self-filling wine goblets, self-trimming lanterns and self-opening temple doors – all ingenious toys. But in his *Mechanics* he dealt with utilitarian devices such as cranes, hoists (lifts) and presses. Another book, *Stereometrica*, gave useful advice on measuring the contents of ships and *amphorae* (jars).

However, Heron perhaps remains best known for his prototype steam engine, a device that was probably of no use at all. In its developed form this was an *aelopile*, a sealed metal cauldron under a hollow metal sphere. Steam funnelled in tubes from the cauldron made the sphere spin, creating the world's first steam turbine Lack of accessible fossil fuels and crude metallurgy may have kept this steam engine a toy, despite legends that it carried fuel up Alexandria's giant *pharos* (lighthouse).

Above and below: Archimedes' most useful invention was his screw. Turned usually by manual labour, it lifted water for irrigation.

MEDICINE
FROM SUPERSTITION TO SCIENCE

Above: Hippocrates (C.460–380BC), the 'father of medicine', was the first to study medicine systematically and scientifically.

Below: Asclepius, the divine healer, treating a patient. Greek medicine never wholly lost its religious connections. From a relief of the 4th century BC.

Both the Hippocratic oath that doctors traditionally swear, and the snake-entwined staff of their profession, reveal medicine's Greek roots. The oath recalls Hippocrates, the 'first doctor', the latter Asclepius and medicine's religious origins. The Greeks pioneered the move from a religious to scientific approach in medical matters, the invention of rational medicine being among their finest deeds.

In Homer's time, Greek attitudes to sickness and medicine mirrored those of Egypt and Babylon. Treatment involved incantations, magical amulets, spells and prayers to Apollo, god of medicine, and his son Asclepius, the divine healer. These customs long persisted, as did *incubation*, sleeping in precincts at Cos sacred to the god, when healing dreams might come in the night. Such psychosomatic methods helped suggestible sufferers. From the 6th century BC, both attitudes and practice began to change, however.

Above: Galen, the great 2nd-century AD physician, believed that human health was governed by the balance of the 'Four Humours'. From a medieval drawing.

HIPPOCRATES, THE 'FATHER OF MEDICINE' (*c.*465–*c.*380BC)

Almost nothing is known of the first true physician, Hippocrates. Traditionally he was associated with the famous medical school on Cos, but surviving buildings there date from after his time and his very existence has been doubted. He probably lived about the same time as Socrates.

Hippocrates first made careful observation of the body the basis of medicine. Though he never practised dissection – which religion discouraged – prayers and sacrifices held no place in his theories. Instead, changes in diet, drugs, rest and keeping the body 'in balance' were key elements of his cure. This rational approach was his greatest single contribution to medicine. About 60 treatises, the *Hippocratic Corpus*, are attributed to him. In *Sacred Disease* he demolished the idea that epilepsy was a god-sent sickness; in *Airs, Waters, Places* he examined the effects of climate and locality on illnesses. Other treatises cover diagnosis, epidemics, paediatrics, nutrition and surgery.

In the 4th century BC Aristotle made a few significant discoveries. His pupil Diocles first practised dissection, so essential to discovering anatomy, and wrote a book on the subject. Dissection of animals was subsequently practised at the Lyceum, Aristotle's school.

ANATOMY IN ALEXANDRIA

In the rich new city of Alexandria, protected by a dynasty of powerful kings with scientific interests and freed from religious taboos, physicians could at last freely practise dissection and even, it is thought, vivisection. Foremost among the bold anatomists of the mid-3rd century BC were Herophilus from Chalcedon and Erasistratus, who had studied at Cos and Athens. Their discoveries about the importance of the heart, brain, vascular and nervous systems were carefully recorded and formed the basis for almost all subsequent medicine for 1,500 years in the Islamic and Christian worlds.

GALEN, THE GREAT SYNTHESIZER (AD129–200)

Galen was a native of Pergamum in Asia Minor. He studied philosophy and rhetoric before switching to study medicine at Pergamum, Smyrna and Alexandria. He began his career treating wounded gladiators at Pergamum. Going to Rome in AD162, he practised as a physician and a medical writer. As the former, he found himself in demand in the highest circles, treating Commodus, the emperor's son, the empress herself and later rulers. Despite fleeing the plague-stricken city in AD166, Galen remained very popular all his life.

As a writer, Galen was prolific. About 350 works are known to be by him. Galen sometimes lectured in public and even dissected pigs' corpses, but original research was not his chief interest. Instead, he tried to synthesize not only earlier findings but also his ideas on philosophy, derived from both Plato and Aristotle, with medicine. A revealing title of one work is *The Ideal Physician is also a Philosopher*.

Galen took a holistic view of health, stressing the importance of exercise, a balanced diet and general hygiene. Among his most vital ideas was the theory of the Four Humours, the four bodily fluids of blood, phlegm, yellow bile and black bile that must be kept in balance. Illness arose when they were out of balance, and might require bloodletting. The overall result was an integrated, comprehensive system summarizing all medical knowledge, canonical until the 17th century.

Above: The Asclepium at Pergamum, in whose sacred precincts patients slept, hoping for healing dreams from the healer-god Asclepius. Such incubation could be very effective with the right person.

Below: Galen's theory of the Four Humours was accepted in Europe and the Arab world for almost 1,500 years.

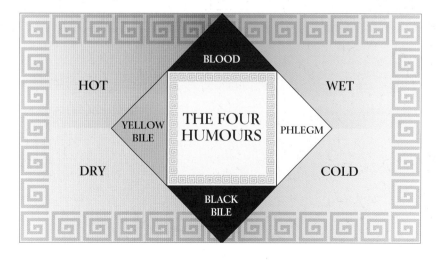

THE FOUR HUMOURS

BLOOD

HOT

WET

YELLOW BILE

PHLEGM

DRY

COLD

BLACK BILE

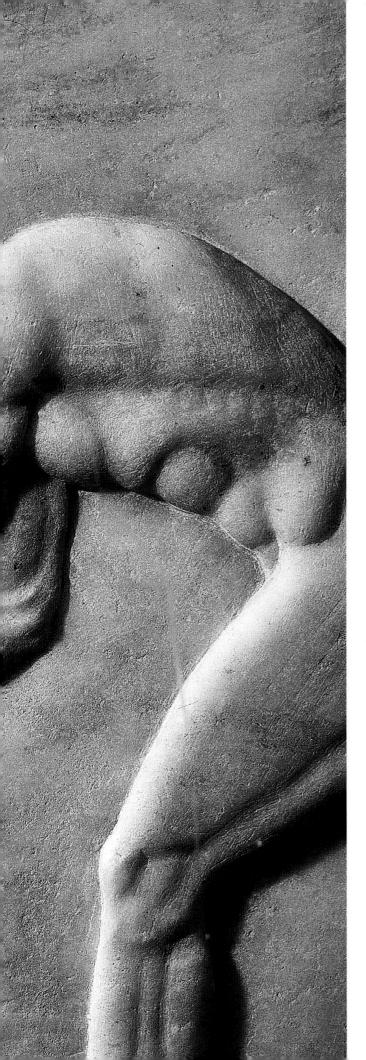

CHAPTER V

ATHLETICS AND SPORT

Athletics, which culminated in the great sporting festivals, were central to Greek life. The *agon* (contest) was crucial to the Greek desire of 'striving always to be best'. Games were important in Homer in the 8th century BC and were still important 1,000 years later under the Romans. While Greek athletic contests are the ancestors of modern sporting events, the differences are as great as the similarities. Greek sports were long dominated by aristocrats, who alone could train properly. Only after 320BC did athletics become professionalized. Contests were between individuals, for there were no team sports. Each polis took intense pride in its victors, honouring them almost as demi-gods.

Excelling in athletics was an expected part of public life for an aspiring aristocrat, as was excelling in oratory or drama. Musical and poetry contests featured in many games, although professional musicians were not admired. Among aspects distinguishing Greek games from other cultures were the nudity of all contestants, which was extremely important – for the gods were shown naked — and the restriction on eligibility to freeborn Greeks from around the Greek world. (Romans were later admitted too, however.) As Greek culture spread around the Mediterranean and Black Sea coasts, and then thinly but widely across Asia after Alexander's conquests, the gymnasium, along with the theatre and agora, became a vital part of urban life.

Left: Two men in the palaestra (wrestling ground), naked like all Greek athletes. From an Athenian carving of c.500BC.

THE GREAT FESTIVALS
THE OLYMPICS AND OTHER GAMES

Above: The starting line of the stadium at Olympia, the site of the most important games in the Hellenic sporting calendar, for which all cities observed a rare truce.

Below: Spartan girls shocked and fascinated other Greeks by exercising only in skimpy tunics, like this girl from the 6th century BC. But they took no part in the main games.

Oldest and most important of Greek festivals, the Olympic Games in honour of Zeus traditionally date from 776BC. Significantly, this was the year at which most Greek cities later chose to start their calendars. According to myth, Hercules was the Games' founder. Olympia's location in the south-western Peloponnese meant that it was distant from major wars (although there were minor local ones) if vulnerable to earthquakes.

The Olympic Games were held quadrennially at the time of the second full moon after the summer solstice. This usually meant late August, not the coolest time of year. Over the centuries Olympia became filled with treasures and fine buildings, the greatest being the Temple of Olympian Zeus. This contained the sculptor Pheidias' last masterpiece, the gold-and-ivory statue of the king of gods, so huge that even seated Zeus' head brushed the roof, making it one of the Seven Wonders of the World. In AD393 Theodosius I banned the Games, whose paganism offended many Christians. (In 1896 the modern Olympics were founded by Pierre de Coubertin.)

THE OLYMPIC TRUCE
A distinctive feature of the Olympics was the proclamation of *Ekecheiria*, the Olympic Truce. Surprisingly, this was almost universally observed and the games were held regularly despite wars and invasions. For their duration, contestants, whether Athenian, Spartan, Theban or Syracusan, recalled they were *all* Greek. To stress this Panhellenism, the ten judges were called *Hellanodikai* (judges of the Greeks). An Olympic prize – a simple olive crown – was the supreme accolade for an athlete.

WOMEN ONLY GAMES
If women could not compete in the main Olympic Games, they had the consolation of holding their own games, the Heraea, honouring the goddess Hera. These too were quadrennial. According to Pausanias writing in the mid 2nd century AD: "The games are footraces for unmarried girls of varying ages. First the youngest run; then come the girls next in age, and the last contestants are the oldest. As they run, their hair falls free and their tunics do not even reach to the knee, while they bare their right shoulders as far as their breasts. The Olympic stadium is reserved for their games but shortened for them by about one-sixth. The winners receive crowns of olive leaves and part of the ox sacrificed to Hera. They may also dedicate statues with their names inscribed upon them." Men were not allowed to watch these games.

Competitors at the games were divided into three age groups: boys, adolescents and grown men. The games were only open to freeborn male Greeks, though from cities all over the Greek world. (Women were barred even from watching). However, there were exceptions. The kings of Macedonia, who claimed Hercules as their ancestor, could participate, but ordinary Macedonians, not classed as Greek, were excluded until after Alexander's conquests.

Later, Roman citizens were also permitted to enter. The most notorious Roman contestant was the emperor Nero, who won *all* the prizes in AD66. Nero introduced Hellenic games to Rome but with little success. The emperor Domitian also failed to interest the Romans in competitive athletics.

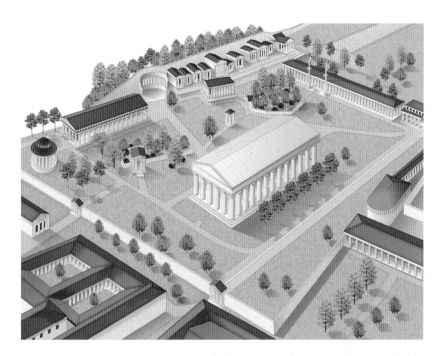

Above: 4th-century BC amphora of runners. The foot races were the oldest and most prestigious games, divided into several types. The original race was for one stadion (185m/ 202 yards), giving its name to the stadium.

FESTIVALS AND GAMES

Other Panhellenic games emulated the Olympics. The most important were the Pythian Games held in honour of Apollo at Delphi – originally every eight years and then, after a reorganization in 582BC, every four years. There were the usual athletic and equestrian events but poetry and music were also important contests. The prize was a wreath of bay leaves, a link to poetry.

The Isthmian Games near Corinth were founded – according to different legends – either by Sisyphus, king of Corinth or by Theseus, king of Athens. A less mythical founder was the Corinthian tyrant Periander in *c.*600BC. The games were held every two years. At the Isthmian Games in 336BC Alexander declared his plan to conquer Persia and there, in 196BC, the Roman general Flaminius proclaimed "liberty for the Greeks", to tumultuous applause. Unfortunately, Roman and Greek ideas of liberty proved very different, leading to prolonged wars.

The Nemean Games, again held every second year, were staged in honour of Zeus at Nemea in the Argolid. They became part of the Panhellenic circuit in 573BC and in the 4th century BC were moved to Argos. The games were similar to those at Olympia.

There were also many local festivals. The grandest were the Panathenaic Games, held every four years as part of the Panathenaic festival in Athena's honour. They included the usual contests but were solely for Athenians.

Above: Aerial view of part of Olympia showing the central Temple of Olympian Zeus and, in the top left corner, the Temple of Hera or Heraion.

Below: The ruins of the covered palaestra (wrestling school) at Olympia date from the 3rd century BC. The site slowly filled with temples, monuments and other buildings donated by kings and cities.

RACES ON FOOT AND BY CHARIOT

Above: An Olympic athlete sprinting for one stadion. From a vase painting of the 4th century BC.

The oldest and most prestigious of the games was the foot race. The word *stadion* (stadium), meaning race course, comes from *stade*, a Greek measurement of 185m (202 yards), the length of the first race on foot. The winner of this inaugural sprint at Olympia gave his name to the Olympiad.

Other foot races developed from this. The two-stade race was traditionally introduced at Olympia in 724BC. The *dolichos* (long race) was introduced in 720BC. Its actual length is uncertain but was probably about 20 stade or 4.8km (3 miles). As in a modern marathon, runners began and ended the race in the stadium, but ran through Olympia itself before returning.

THE HOPLITE RACE

Below: Chariot racing was the most glamorous, expensive and dangerous of the contests. It brought huge glory to the victor, although he often employed a driver who might be a slave. From a red figure vase of the 6th century BC.

The last running contest added to the Olympics was the *hoplitodromos* (hoplite race), in 520BC. Contestants ran around the stadium for 1.6km (1 mile), carrying a shield with greaves (leg guards) and helmet. As their armour weighed up to 24kg (60lb), runners often dropped their shields or tripped over fallen competitors, making onlookers laugh. In vase paintings, runners are sometimes shown leaping over the fallen shields of their collapsing competitors as they pass them.

This race flaunted each polis' military strength. As in hoplite warfare, stamina counted for more than speed, the Spartans being particularly good at the hoplitodromos, as was to be expected from Greece's best hoplites. The link between sport and military training was always acknowledged by the Greeks.

CHARIOT RACING

The most expensive and dangerous Olympic contest was chariot racing, which only rich aristocrats or kings could afford. Chariots had long been used for racing – Homer describes chariot racing at Patroclus' funeral in *The Iliad*.

The sport was introduced to the Olympics in 680BC and soon eclipsed horse racing. Chariots were very light wooden two-wheeled vehicles, drawn by two or four horses. They were difficult to control but the glory and prize went not to the skilled and courageous charioteer, who might be a slave, but to the owner.

This was the one race in which the contestants were not nude but wore a long robe. Falling to the ankles, it fastened high at the waist with a plain belt. Two straps crossing high at the back prevented this from ballooning during the race. Like modern jockeys, charioteers were chosen for their light build.

Arcesilaus IV, king of Greek Cyrene (in Libya), won the chariot race at the Pythian Games at Delphi in 462BC. His slave driver was in fact the only one to complete the whole course. In 416BC the flamboyant Athenian aristocrat Alcibiades had seven chariots in one race at Olympia, which came in first, second and fourth. Philip II of Macedon entered and won an Olympic chariot race in 356BC, a victory that helped prove his true Hellenic credentials.

DANGEROUS GLAMOUR

Chariot races were notoriously dangerous, sometimes lethal. Each race began with a procession into the hippodrome, a herald proclaiming the drivers' and owners' names. About 550m (600 yards) long, the course at Olympia could take

60 chariots but normally fewer entered. The four-horse race – run anticlockwise – had 12 laps, with sharp turns around the posts at each end.

A vivid, perhaps eyewitness, description of the Pythian races comes in Sophocles' play *Electra*, in which the exiled Orestes takes part: "As the bronze trumpet sounded they were off, all shouting to their horses and urging them on… The clatter of rattling chariots filled the arena, the dust flew up as they raced along in a dense mass, each driver goading his team mercilessly trying to draw clear of rival axles and panting horses, whose steaming breath and sweat drenched the flying wheels with foam…

"Orestes kept his horse near the pillar at each end so skilfully that his hub just grazed the turning-post by a hair's breadth each time… But at the last bend he misjudged it, slackening his left rein before the horse was safely round, and so hit the post. The hub was smashed across and he was hurled over the chariot rail, entangled in the reins. As he fell, his horses ran madly on around the course… he was dragged along the ground, his legs pointing at the sky, until other charioteers stopped his horses and released him, so bloody that none of his friends could have recognized him."

Chariot racing, unlike most Greek sports, proved hugely popular in Rome The Circus Maximus, the largest building in Rome, reputedly held 250,000 people. Later, chariot racing was transplanted to Constantinople, capital of the Christian Byzantine Empire, somehow escaping Christian censure. The emperor's palace had a passage leading directly into the hippodrome, so central was chariot racing to Byzantine life. But the rioting mobs who supported the rival Green and Blue factions in Byzantium had long forgotten the ideals of the Classical agon.

Left: The hoplitodromos (hoplite race) was added to the Olympics in 520BC. Contestants ran around the stadium for 1,600m (1 mile) in full armour.

Below: The Charioteer of Delphi, *a rare surviving bronze masterpiece of serene beauty, from c.473BC.*

LIGHT AND HEAVY SPORTS

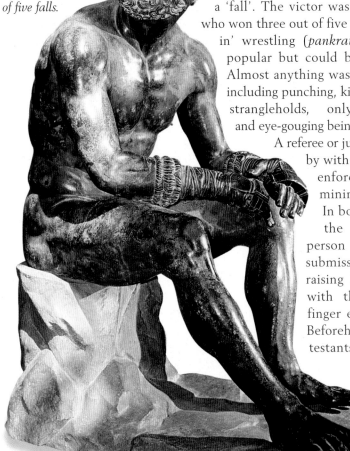

Above: Athletes wrestling, from a red figure vase attributed to the Euergides painter, an Attic artist of the 5th century BC. In wrestling, a contestant tried to immobilize his opponent, either by getting him in a hold or pinning him to the ground in a 'fall'. A victor won by getting three out of five falls.

Other sports included boxing and wrestling, both classed as 'heavy' sports, and the long jump and throwing the javelin or discus, considered 'light'. The pentathlon, which was considered by Aristotle the best of sports, combined all five. But all were individual contests. This was the one major difference between ancient and modern athletics: team sports of any sort, were quite unknown in Greece, that land of herocially ultra-competitive individuals.

BOXING AND WRESTLING

In wrestling (*pale*) the aim was to immobilize your opponent, either by getting him in a hold or pinning him to the ground in a 'fall'. The victor was the man who won three out of five falls. 'All-in' wrestling (*pankration*) was popular but could be brutal. Almost anything was allowed, including punching, kicking and strangleholds, only biting and eye-gouging being banned. A referee or judge stood by with a stick to enforce these minimal rules. In both sports the defeated person signalled submission by raising his hand with the index finger extended. Beforehand, contestants rubbed themselves down with oil and sprinkled sand over their naked bodies. They also tried to soften the sun-baked earth by breaking it up or, in the case of the pankration, soaking it in water. This made the resulting bout a mud bath.

Boxing was even more dangerous. There were no 'Queensberry rules' to restrict where blows might land, and most were aimed at the head. Rabbit punches and blows with the butt of the hand were common. Boxers wore leather thongs around their hands, which later were iron-weighted.

Bouts were decided by a knockout, and often lasted hours. On rare occasions this could lead to the death of one contestant. In that case, however, the prize went to the dead man and his opponent was banned from contests for life. Boxers with their battered faces were notoriously ugly, and therefore not so widely admired as most other athletes.

'LIGHT' SPORTS

The long jump, which seems to have been the only Greek jumping contest, differed radically from the modern long jump. Contestants carried weights of up to 4.5kg (10lb), which they swung forward to increase their mid-air momentum. They reached lengths of 16.6m (54ft), possibly not in one single leap but in a series of rabbit-like jumps. Running remained one of the events at the Panhellenic games such as the Pythian, but the other 'light' sports were performed only as parts of the pentathlon.

The discus thrown by Greek athletes varied considerably in its weight, but as all competitors at a particular festival used

Left: A statue of Apollonius, a famous boxer. In the Hellenistic period (322–30BC) successful professional athletes could become celebrities.

FAMOUS ATHLETES

The cult of the victor was a striking aspect of the Panhellenic games. Winners were hailed as godlike heroes in their home towns. Statues were raised to them, poetry written in their honour – some of it, such as Pindar's, very fine – breaches were even made in the city walls to welcome them on their return. Down to *c*.400BC most victors were aristocrats because they alone could devote themselves to almost full-time training. From the 4th century BC athletes who were not nobly born began to rival these blue-blooded sportsmen. Later still, professional athletes in the modern sense became common.

Typical of an early victor was Milon of Croton in southern Italy. He won the Olympic wrestling prize several times in a career that began with winning the boys' contest in 540BC and lasted 26 years. When finally defeated by a younger man, he was carried shoulder-high around the stadium to cheers. Renowned for his strength, Milon was also known for his immense appetite. The boxer Melancomas of Caria became famous not only for his powerful body but also for his unusual technique. He preferred not to hit his opponents but instead to wear them out by dodging their blows.

Above: A youthful discobolus (disc-thrower). From a black figure vase attributed to the 'Epeleius Painter', c.480BC.

the same one, this did not matter. Surviving examples, made from marble, bronze or lead, weigh between 1.5 and 6.5kg (3 and 14lb), with diameters ranging from approximately 17 to 35cm (6 to 14 inches).

Javelins for athletes differed from the military javelins, being made of an extremely light elder-wood. They had throwing loops that made them spin in flight, keeping them on course. Throws of up to 92m (100 yards) were achievable, sources suggest.

THE PENTATHLON

The pentathlon combined all five sports: discus and javelin throwing, long jump, running and wrestling. It was considered the supreme test of an athlete, for it tested stamina, strength and speed. It was added in 708BC to the 18th Olympiad.

According to legend it was invented by Jason (who had earlier led the Argonauts on the Quest for the Golden Fleece). He combined the five contests, awarding the first prize to his friend Peleus, the father of Achilles, Homer's super-hero. The historical order of events is uncertain, as is how the prizes were awarded. Probably the winner of at least three parts of the overall contest won the pentathlon.

The Victorian British, with their ideals of fair play and the 'game being the thing', on looking at Greek athletics, fondly imagined they had found like-minded precursors. In reality most Greek athletes competed with the obsessive determination of modern professional athletes, although they seldom became rich by doing so.

Below: Athletes with a discus and a javelin. From a red figure vase of the 4th century BC. Both discus and javelin-throwing were considered 'light sports'.

THE GYMNASIUM AND PALAESTRA

Above: The 'Gladiators' Gymnasium' at Pompeii in Italy. The gymnasium, central to true Hellenic life, was adopted by many non-Greek cities too, if for different ends.

Below: Athletes being presented with victory tokens, from an Athenian red figure cup of the 5th century BC. Victorious athletes received only symbolic prizes but gained immense prestige.

The *gymnasion* (gymnasium) and the *palaestra* (wrestling ground) were as central to Greek life as the agora or temples. They were far more than modern gyms or fitness centres, serving as clubs and centres of social and cultural life.

In the gymnasia and palaestras of Athens, Socrates discoursed to Athens' brightest youth in the 5th century BC. Later, Plato and Aristotle founded their schools, the Academy and Lyceum, near gymnasia. These were built outside the city because they needed so much land. (Plato himself had been a wrestler in his youth). The ruins of the gymnasium at Ai Khanum in Afghanistan, a Greek city founded by Alexander the Great or his successors (perhaps originally an Alexandria), bear as quotations from Aristotle the maxims for the Five Ages of Man. Dating from *c.*200BC, these show that, even here, thousands of miles from Greece, the link between mental and physical exercise remained strong.

> ### THE IMPORTANCE OF NUDITY
> The word *gymnasion* comes from *gymnos*, naked, for all athletes exercised and competed nude. Athletes at the Olympics and other games always participated nude, the perfect state in which Greek artists depicted gods and heroes. This stress on nudity distinguishes Greek culture from all others. Even the Romans, in so many ways the Greeks' heirs, did not share this love of idealized nudity (although Romans at times exercised naked). Male nudity, openly admired, probably increased the general homoerotic aura of athletics.

THE PERFECT MALE BODY
The gymnasium was essentially a public sports ground open to all citizens. Usually stoas were built around the sanded area, originally a running track, where those not exercising could talk or ogle the athletes. In classical Athens there were private gymnasia, some socially exclusive. The politician Themistocles, mastermind of Persia's defeat in 480BC, had to join an un-smart gymnasium, but this suited his democratic instincts well.

Most cities established and maintained at least one public gymnasium. Citizens' physical fitness was seen as vital to the health of the city itself – unsurprisingly, as a polis relied for its existence on the fighting abilities of its citizen army. Socrates, in a dialogue written by Xenophon (a soldier), chided Epigenes, another disciple, for not keeping in good shape, for shirking his duty as a citizen: "You've got the body of someone who just doesn't care about public matters... You should care for your body like an Olympic athlete." In Athens, gymnasia were supervised by boards of ten *gymnasiarchs* (superintendents), one from each tribe. In smaller poleis an honorary gymnasiarch hired professional trainers. Lucian, writing in the 2nd century AD, summed up the Greek ideal: "The young men have a tanned complexion from the sun ... they reveal spirit, fire and manliness. They are in fabulous condition, being neither lean and skinny nor excessively fat, but have perfectly symmetrical bodies." This perfectly describes the *Doryphorus* statue made by Polyclitus 650 years earlier, long a canon of male beauty.

PALAESTRA AND BATHS

Sometimes adjacent to the gymnasium but often separate, the palaestra or wrestling ground was similarly laid out as a rectangular court surrounded by stoas, often thicker on the north side to protect against winter winds.

More compact than a gymnasium, a palaestra might be found inside the city, which increased its attraction as a social and intellectual centre. Before wrestling or boxing, athletes covered themselves with olive oil – a costly procedure, at times subsidized by public funds – and dusted themselves with fine sand. This gave some protection against the sun or wind. Younger men who could afford to spent much of the day toning up their bodies and, sometimes, their minds. Boys received most of their physical education in the paleastra's stoas, ogled by older men and watched over by their tutor (usually a slave), who was intended to deter would-be seducers.

After exercising, athletes scraped off their sweat, oil and dust with a strigal, a metal object, or a sponge. The Greeks had public baths that, if not luxurious like the Romans' opulent structures, had hip baths, a hot room and a communal plunge pool.

Above: The palaestra at Olympia, the most prestigious in the Greek world. Here contestants for the great quadrennial games did their final training.

Left: Polyclitus of Argos's Doryphorus *(Spear-carrier), incarnating the perfectly honed, symmetrical Greek ideal. A Roman copy of the bronze original by the great 5th-century BC sculptor.*

CHAPTER VI

WORK AND LEISURE

Greece's cultural brilliance rested on a very limited economic base. Greece has few fertile valleys. Much land is rough hill terrain, although Sicily and some other colonies were more fertile. Later, Alexander's conquests opened up wide new territories but widened the gap between rich and poor. Life for most Greeks, if frugal, was lived with passionate intensity. The Greeks celebrated marriages, funerals and other events with ceremony, almost always in the open. The idea of a private life was considered eccentrically antisocial – a charge levelled against the playwright Euripides when he retreated to Salamis Island. Women, however, remained at home most of the time, especially in Athens. Closeted in cramped houses, they enjoyed little freedom except in religious roles. Such seclusion may partly explain the prevalence of male homo-sexuality, which in Classical Greece enjoyed a status probably unique in history. But the monogamous family was the basis of society.

Not unique to ancient Greece, but hard for the modern world to accept, was the prevalence of slavery. Slavery in the Greek world lacked any racist element – one source of slaves was other Greeks – but it alone made possible the leisured life, whether devoted to athletics, politics, art, drama or philosophy. The Greeks' achievement in these fields distinguishes them from other, often richer, slave-owning societies such as Carthage, which is famed for little beyond its wealth.

Left: 6th-century BC cup of a man embracing a woman, probably a hetaera (courtesan). Greek artists celebrated all aspects of life.

FARMERS, SHEPHERDS AND FISHERMEN

Paradoxically, while Greek life was urban and focused on the polis, most citizens remained farmers, except in the rare trading city such as Corinth, which had little hinterland. Most farmer-citizens lived inside their polis for reasons of security and entertainment, commuting out to their fields. However, some built solid shelters in the countryside for the busy summer months. Land always retained its unique social, political and symbolic status as the basis of wealth.

SKILLED FARMERS

Greek farms were mostly very small, with a typical plot being only 6ha (15 acres). Technically, farming always remained simple, but within these limits Greek farmers exploited their land to the full. They multi-cropped their fields, mixing many different crops – vegetables including pulses, fruits, figs, vines and olives – and

Above: Two men threshing wheat by hand. Farming in Greece was traditionally small-scale, providing small surpluses even in good years.

Below: Despite most Greek cities' proximity to the sea, fish remained something of a rarity – if one much enjoyed, as this exuberant marine mosaic from Pompeii suggests.

FISH, A RARE DISH

Most Greek cities were near the sea, so fish might be thought to have been a staple food. But although authors mention fish-eating, and fishbones have often been unearthed, fish usually remained a relative luxury. The Mediterranean is not a particularly rich area for fishing. Without modern means of transport and storage, fish had to be eaten right away. This meant that the Greeks only ate fish occasionally and in small amounts, often only to add flavour to otherwise monotonous meals.

---

also letting fields lie fallow. They normally grew fruit and vegetables in plots close to town, while up on the hills shepherds tended flocks of sheep and goats. Transhumance was practised: moving animals up to mountain pastures in summer and back again in winter, so that their dung fertilized the land. Owners of such flocks were among the wealthier minority of farmers, however.

HARD TOIL

Greek rural life was far from idyllic. Described in *The Iliad* and more fully in Hesiod's *Works and Days*, it was for most people a daily grind. Better-off farmers had oxen, which could pull carts as well as ploughs but needed feeding and watering year round, plus a slave or two. Slaves provided more skilled muscle-power but needed feeding *and* clothing all year round. Both human and non-human live-stock represented major investments.

In the 6th century BC Greek farmers – except those in poor backwoods like Aetolia – were pulled into a 'market economy', a process speeded up by the introduction of coinage. Because early coins were high-value pieces, barter

Left: Greek sheep-farmers often practised transhumance, moving flocks up to the mountains in summer and back to the lowlands in winter, where they multi-cropped with olive groves. Sheep dung is a valuable fertilizer.

remained the norm for daily purposes, but wealth could now be measured and amassed. While the rich grew richer, the poor became ever more indebted, often being forced to make their own persons surety for debts, so losing their liberty along with their land.

To protect poorer farmers, in 594BC the Athenian reformer Solon banned enslavement for debt and the export of wheat from Attica. This led to an enduring enthusiasm for cultivating olive trees. It needed to endure, for olive trees take 15 years to start bearing fruit and about 40 to become fully productive. Attic olive oil was valued across the Mediterranean as a perfume as well as for cooking and lighting. The vases in which it was sold encouraged the phenomenal growth of Athenian pottery. Wheat was now imported to Attica from the Black Sea area or Egypt.

THE STAPLE CROPS

Barley and wheat were the main cereals grown in Greece. Olive groves allowed intercropping, i.e. land could be cultivated beneath or between the trees, but olives cannot stand much frost. Vines, tougher and thriving on very rocky slopes, were even more widely planted. Wine was the main drink after water, a useful (if unrecognized) source of sugar and vitamins. Pulses formed a key part of the diet, and helped fix nitrogen in the soil. Cabbages, onions, garlic and lettuce were grown widely, but tomatoes, rice, peppers and potatoes were unknown. Figs, apples, grapes, plums and quinces were common

fruits, but meat was an expensive rarity for ordinary people. Cheese, from sheep, goats and cattle, was eaten more often.

PERENNIAL SHORTAGES

The Greek climate is hard for farmers. Rainfall, mostly concentrated in the winter months, can vary dramatically from year to year and place to place. As Aristotle noted in his treatise on *Meteorology*: "At times drought or flood can affect large areas of the country simultaneously, but sometimes it has only local effects. Often the country overall has the normal rainfall for the season or even more, but one part suffers drought. Occasionally the opposite happens, when the country all around has only light rainfall or even a drought, one particular part is deluged in rain." Farming produced small surpluses in good years, and in bad years there were acute shortages.

Below: The olive harvest from a black figure vase. Olives were vital to Greek life, providing oil for cooking and lighting and serving also as a soap-substitute.

TRADERS AND TRADE ROUTES

Above: Most merchants ships remained small with one mast. Despite this, Greek traders criss-crossed the Mediterranean and the Black Sea. From a vase of c.500BC.

Mycenaean traders had crossed the Mediterranean from Sicily to Egypt, but they disappeared after 1200BC. By the 8th century BC, Greece's modest trade was dominated by Phoenician ships. Yet soon after, as growing populations pressed on limited land, Greek poleis began to found colonies around the Mediterranean and Black Sea. Trade was seldom the chief reason for this expansion – Naucratis in Egypt was one of the few colonies founded for trade – but good harbours were always sought. Even colonies founded as agricultural settlements initially needed goods from the homeland. Transport was always far cheaper by sea than land for heavy goods.

Pottery, at first mostly from Corinth but by the mid-6th century BC overwhelmingly from Athens, was Greece's main export. Black and red figure vases containing olive oil from Attica and fine wines – from Chios, Samos, Thasos and Lesbos, where the poet Sappho's brother was a wine merchant – went to Egypt, Italy and Gaul (France). But the Greeks also made other, even grander containers.

A PRINCESS'S TOMB

Herodotus in his *Histories* mentioned a *krater* (bronze jar) holding 300 amphorae of wine, made by Laconian smiths for Croesus of Lydia (560–546BC). He was thought to have exaggerated until the discovery in 1953 of a vessel at Vix in an Iron Age tomb in central France. The *Krater of Vix*, the largest known ancient bronze vessel, is 1.5m (5ft) high and could have held about 1,089 litres (240 gallons) of wine. Along with Athenian silver cups c.530 and 520BC, it was buried in the tomb of a Gallic princess around 500BC. It shows how Greek trade had already penetrated distant lands.

Massilia (Marseilles), founded c.600BC by settlers from Ionia, became the chief entrepôt for this trade. Gaul, on the overland routes north, was by 500BC very important to the Greeks as Carthage had closed the south-western Mediterranean to monopolize trade with northwest Europe.

THE GRAIN TRADE

During the course of the 6th century, Athens, growing fast, became critically dependent on grain imports from the Black Sea. The fertile Ukrainian and

Left: The Krater of Vix, *the largest known ancient bronze vessel, which can hold c.1,089 litres (240 gallons), shows the extent of Greek exports. Unearthed in Burgundy, central France, it dates from c.520BC.*

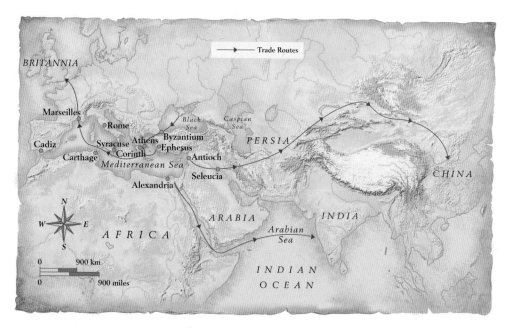

Left: Greek trade routes spread right across the Mediterranean and the Black Sea, exchanging Greek artefacts usually for wheat. After Alexander the Great, these routes extended far across central Asia and then down the Red Sea to India.

Russian steppes were then ruled by Scythian princes. Fortunately, they proved fond of the Greek wine, oil, pottery and other artefacts sold them in return for their exports of hides, timber, slaves and grain. Safeguarding the wheat route became a prime concern of Athenian politics from the time of the Pisistratids (545–510BC). Hence the importance of controlling the Hellespont and Bosphorus.

The Piraeus, rebuilt on the gridiron pattern after the Persian wars (490–478BC) by Hippodamus, became the greatest port in the eastern Mediterranean, secured to Athens by the Long Walls. An import-export tax of just 2 per cent made it an attractive place to do business, including banking, and many Greeks from ravaged Ionia settled there.

ROUTES ACROSS ASIA

After Alexander's conquest of the Persian Empire, new overland routes east opened up. In great Hellenistic cities such as Antioch or Alexandria, the rich demanded luxuries: perfumes, silks, drugs, spices and precious stones. Spices came from India and Arabia Felix (Yemen). Silk from China remained a great luxury even in the Roman Empire, as China jealously guarded its monopoly of seri-culture. A rougher 'wild silk' came from the island of Cos. Caravan routes along the valleys of Asia Minor made coastal cities like Ephesus and Miletus wealthy.

The Ptolemaic rulers of Egypt encouraged exploration, sending expeditions up the Nile in search of gold and ivory and down the Red Sea looking for spices. This second route led to a lucky discovery in 116BC, when a sea captain in their service found the sea-route to India via the Red Sea port of Berenice. Utilizing the regular monsoon winds that blow across the Indian Ocean, he set sail in July, returning home blown by reverse winds in December. The routes east were outlined in the *Periplus Maris Erythrae*, a handbook for sailors of the 1st century AD.

Below: After 550BC Athens became increasingly dependent on grain imports from the Black Sea region. Safeguarding the wheat route through the Hellespont (Dardanelles), here shown at Gallipoli, became very important in Athenian politics.

TRADES AND PROFESSIONS
FROM POTTERS TO BANKERS

Although Greek society always remained mostly agricultural, craftsmen had a recognized role by classical times in large cities such as Athens and Corinth. Even in the Bronze Age, Cretan potters and goldsmiths had produced fine artefacts exported around the Aegean and sometimes farther afield. A bronze tripod made in Crete is mentioned by the tablets in Linear B, an early form of Greek. One was found in the palace at Pylos, dating from *c*.1200BC. The ensuing Dark Ages ended such trade, which revived only after 700BC. Athens most notably then became, and long remained, noted for making goods of superb quality.

POTTERY
The most common Greek artefact is pottery. Pottery shards have the advantage (for archaeologists) of being almost indestructible. When reassembled, vases make a valuable guide to dating because styles changed fairly quickly and consistently. Olive oil and wine from Greece were almost always exported in pottery amphorae. The superb vases, often signed by their makers or found intact in Etruscan tombs, such as the *Chigi Vase* with its triple tier of friezes from *c*.620BC, were certainly regarded as artworks, not just as containers. However, with plastic unknown and glass rare and expensive, most storage vessels and domestic appliances, from cookers to hip-baths, were made of fired clay.

Corinth, which initially dominated the important carrying trade west, was home to the first great ceramicists. Then, in the mid-6th century BC, Athenian potters almost totally displaced them. From the late 5th century BC on they, in turn, faced rivalry from Boeotian and southern Italian potters. But booming demand kept all Greek potters busy. Other cities specialized in different products: Chalcis and Corinth in metalware, Miletus in textiles, Pergamum later in parchment. Potters in Athens originally worked in the Kerameikos, the potters' quarter (our word ceramic comes from Greek *keramikos*) south-west of the Agora. The hill on the west of the Agora, the Kolonos Agoraeus, was known for its concentration of blacksmiths and bronze-workers. The whole area must have rung with the sounds of hammered metal, with smoke from their charcoal forges forming a mini-smog. Appropriately, the temple on the low hill nearby was dedicated to Hephaestus, the blacksmith god.

CEPHALUS, SHIELD-MAKER EXTRAORDINARY
Later, the Piraeus, which became after 480BC the economic heart of Athens – indeed soon almost of the eastern Mediterranean – attracted numerous merchants and workshops. Many different types of craftsmen, free or slave, including bronze-, silver- and goldsmiths, cobblers, carpenters, and arms and armour makers, lived and worked there.

Above: Storage jars for olive oil from the Bronze Age. Oil was always one of the Greeks' main tradeable commodities.

Below right: Vase painting of a smith at work. Whether free or slave, all smiths worked in small forges, mass production being unknown.

Below: Marble stele (gravestone) of Sosinos of Gortyna, a bronze founder of the late 5th century BC. Classical Athens attracted many such specialized metal-workers.

Left: The Temple of Hephaestus, the god of metalworkers, overlooked the Agora, the centre of Athens' social and economic life. Nearby was the smiths' quarter.

Below: A potter of the late 6th century BC, *the period when Athenian ceramic products became pre-eminent around the Mediterranean.*

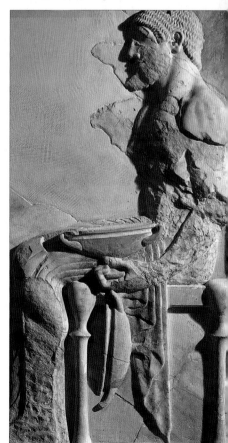

One of the largest workshops known in the Piraeus belonged to Cephalus, a wealthy metic (resident foreigner) from Syracuse. He appears in the opening passages of Plato's great dialogue *Republic*. Cephalus was a historical figure, the owner of 120 slaves who specialized in making shields – an essential part of the Athenian war effort, the dialogue being set during the Peloponnesian War. However, these slaves were probably not all under one roof and certainly were not working on a production line. Instead, each would have made a whole shield himself. Cephalus was among the richest men in Athens. Socrates, Plato's protagonist in the dialogue, treats him with respect, so clearly tradesmen as such were not despised even by aristocrats such as Plato. Most workshops had a maximum of five or six workers.

BANKERS AND MONEY-LENDERS

Banking in Greece was originally a monopoly of the temples. People would deposit and borrow money on interest from priests, and temples remained important safe deposits for major sums until the end of paganism. But, when coins became common in the 5th century BC, money-lenders called *trapezitae* set up their 'tables' in public places such as the South Stoa in Athens, displacing most temples. (Greek *trapeza*, bank, comes from *trapeza* 'table', just as bank comes from Latin *bancus*, 'bench'.) This banking system operated primarily on letters of credit, not coinage. Pasion, an ex-slave, was one of the richest bankers of the 4th century BC. Another system was later developed by Ionian cities such as Miletus, where financial transactions became so complicated that they required professional managers. Often these worked with the city authorities to create an effective bank monopoly.

In Ptolemaic Egypt, where commerce on a grander scale required larger funds, a central state monopoly bank was established in Alexandria. It opened branches across the kingdom and continued in operation under Roman rule after 30BC.

DRINKING TOGETHER
SYMPOSIA AND BARS

For Greek men, a symposium was the great occasion for socializing. *Symposion* means literally 'drinking together', and wine (the only alcohol the Greeks drank) flowed at these events. They could be celebrations – of an athletic or artistic victory – but many seemed to have just involved people dropping in uninvited. A true symposium was more than a mere booze-up. It offered, besides food, entertainment by dancers and flute girls, who were enjoyed as much for looks as their music. At the best type of symposium, wine-fired conversation was what finally counted.

A symposium took place in a house's *andron* ('men's room'), a special window-less room on the ground floor. Its floor was raised at the walls, against which couches were arranged. Greeks always dined reclining on couches, a custom copied by Etruscans and Romans. Guests on arrival had their sandals

Above: Pompeii fresco showing Ariadne seduced by Dionysus, the re-enactment of which myth in Xenophon's Symposium *fired onlookers with heterosexual lust.*

removed by slaves and might be garlanded with flowers and anointed before being shown to their couches. Two men shared one couch, reclining on their left sides. Finger bowls were placed on tables beside them – the Greeks ate chiefly with their fingers, throwing bones to the floor for the dogs.

THE SYMPOSIARCH
A crucial figure at a well-run symposium was the *symposiarch*, master of ceremonies, elected for the evening. He decided the proportion of wine to water. This varied, but about two parts of wine to five of water was usual. (Drinking wine undiluted was thought barbaric if not insane. Conversely Demosthenes, the great orator, was thought a prig for preferring plain water.) The two were mixed in a krater, a large elaborate bowl, snow sometimes first being used to cool

Above: Diners at a symposium from a mural in the Tomb of the Diver, Poseidonia (Paestum), Italy, c.480BC. Symposia were among the highlights of Greek life, where conversation and entertainment, high or low, accompanied the wine.

Below: A scene from a symposium, where two diners, sharing a couch as was usual, seem drunk and mutually attracted. From a red figure Attic vase of c.500BC.

the wine in a *psyketer* (wine-cooler). Guests decided how many kraters of wine to prepare, as all drank the same amount. At most symposia, three kraters were thought enough. In the words of Eubulus, a playwright, "One krater is for health, one for love, one for sleep."

Wine circulated 'from left to right', i.e. anticlockwise, the symposiarch setting the pace. Libations – sprinkling wine on the floor – were made to Dionysus, the wine god, Zeus and to the special *agathon daimon*, the good spirit presiding. As wine flowed, diners might debate agreed topics, but there were other entertainments too.

FLUTE GIRLS AND PHILOSOPHY

In an atmosphere as enclosed as a modern nightclub's, with wine flowing ever more freely, diners played games such as *kottabos*, flicking wine at a target. Sex – with other guests, or more usually with dancing girls and serving boys (both often slaves) – might follow. Illustrations show some symposia degenerating into orgies.

But two famous dinner parties ended very differently. In Plato's novel-like *Symposium*, the guests – among them Aristophanes and the tragedian Agathon, the host – solemnly if not soberly discuss the nature of *eros*, sexual desire. Alcibiades bursts in drunk, takes over the symposiarch's role and falls asleep after wailing that Socrates seems as impervious to sex as he is to the effects of drink. The crux of the dialogue comes in Socrates' report of a talk with Diotima, a priestess, about the higher eros, ideally homoerotic, that engenders ideas, not bodies.

In *Symposium* by Xenophon, another of Socrates' disciples, an evening ends with an "imitation of the wedding-night of Dionysus and Ariadne… When the guests saw that 'Dionysus' was attractive and 'Ariadne' gorgeous, and the actors were not playing but really kissing, they

Right: Playing kottabos, a game in which wine was flicked across the room at small statuettes by diners. From a late 5th-century BC *krater (drinking cup).*

became fired up… When they finally saw the actors apparently going to bed together, the bachelors swore they must get married and the married men rode off on their horses to their wives with but one purpose in mind." The eroticism here is wholly heterosexual.

BARS AND TAVERNS

Poorer citizens could not afford such festivities and had to socialize elsewhere in a bar or tavern called *kapeleion*. If some *kapeleia* were only stalls, others were many-roomed buildings. Citizens could eat snacks and buy wine in flasks to take away along with torches to light their way home through Athens' unlit streets.

Kapeleia were often condemned as sources of popular disturbance and riots, rather like pubs in modern Britain.

Above: A flute girl entertaining men at a symposium, a typical entertainment. From a red figure vase of c.450BC.

GREEK SEXUALITY
ACTS AND ATTITUDES

Ancient Greece was once seen as a sexual arcadia where happy pagans, free from Christian restraint, enjoyed sex in ways damned by the Bible or law. In particular, homosexuality, male and female, was openly celebrated. Such views of Greece as a homosexual paradise owe as much to

Left: 6th-century BC herm, a phallic good luck sign placed outside houses and at street-corners, originally dedicated to the god Hermes. Male nudity in all its forms was much celebrated by Greek art, encouraging or reflecting Greek homoeroticism.

Below: A man embracing a boy. Such paederastia (pederasty) was thought acceptable, even admirable, if the relationship was between social equals and suitably conducted. From a red figure cup by the 'Briseis Painter'.

fantasy as to reality. The Greeks had no words for, or concepts of, 'homosexual' or 'heterosexual' (terms coined in the late 19th century), nor for 'gay', which gained its current meaning even more recently. They would have thought people who so defined themselves as odd, bisexuality being the unspoken norm.

The Greeks did, however, have a word for *paederastia*, pederasty, the love of an adult man for boy – usually an adolescent. Far from regarding this as a crime, classical art and literature celebrated an idealized paederastia. This fact, which so embarrassed Victorian scholars, must be seen in the context of the Greeks' general attitudes to love and sex.

CONCEPTS OF 'LOVE'

For us 'love' means romantic love in the St Valentine's Day sense: couples – mainly if not always heterosexual – love each other physically and spiritually and aim to live 'happily ever after' together. Tragedy arises when requited love is blocked, as in *Romeo and Juliet*. Things were very different in antiquity.

Greek men were often fond of their wives. Certainly they felt a duty and responsibility to them. But they did not usually marry for love, marriages being arranged for social reasons. (Spouses presumably felt sexual desire for each other – the Greek birth-rate was certainly high enough.) Families were the acknowledged bedrock of any polis, essential to sustaining Greek society.

In contrast, eros, overwhelming sexual desire, was seen as a 'bitter-sweet' disruptive force, at times terrifyingly destructive, especially if it afflicted women. When eros strikes women in Greek myth and tragedy, the results are often catastrophic: the Trojan War was caused by the headstrong love of Helen for Prince Paris; Queen Clytemnestra, for the

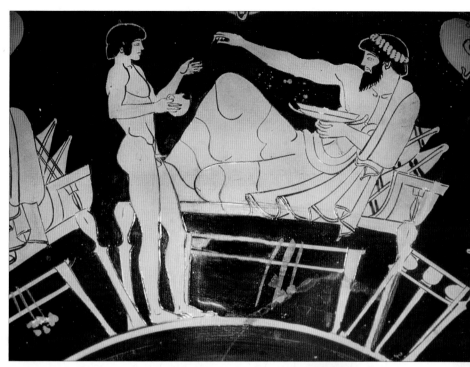

Right: Red-figure painting of a man being served by a naked youth – perhaps a slave – at a symposium. Symposia could end with the diners having sex with the slaves, male or female.

sake of her lover, murders her husband Agamemnon on his return from Troy, before being killed by her son Orestes; Phaedra, King Theseus' wife, conceives an unrequited passion for her stepson Hippolytus that leads to the deaths of both. No happy endings here.

Philosophers attempted self-control to gain *eudaimonia* (contentment) or *ataraxia* (stoical indifference) to escape sexual turmoil. Others, less high-minded, tried to possess the object of their desire, male or female, as swiftly as possible.

A HOMOEROTIC WORLD?

Every Greek city boasted a second marble and bronze population of athletes, heroes and gods. These statues portrayed idealized men with superb bodies, mostly naked. Balancing this Olympian idealism were statues of herms, phallic symbols topped by heads. While the city overflowed with male nudity, female statues, naked or clothed, were far less frequent, although beautiful nude goddesses were sculpted from the 4th century BC.

This possibly roused any latent homoerotic feelings. More crucially, unmarried Greek women were so secluded that young men hardly ever met them. Young girls, being uneducated, may have been uninspiring company. Nor were married women a better prospect. Adultery, according to an old Draconian law, was a capital offence. Unsurprisingly, many men turned to prostitutes, but some preferred other males, usually teenaged boys.

LOVER AND BELOVED

In the ideal homoerotic relationship, the *erastes*, a lover in his twenties, courted an *eromenos*, the beloved, a boy in his teens of similar social status. The gymnasium was a common meeting place, where each could admire the other working out naked. A boy received small gifts from his

admirer – a hare or cockerel – but was expected to behave with suitable modesty, rather as 'respectable' girls being courted in the West were once expected to behave. Any hint of effeminacy on either side was strongly deplored.

How much actual sex occurred remains debatable. Ancient authors tend to discretion, modern ones to speculation. But one thing is clear: such relationships were not viewed by either partner as degrading, for soon the eromenos would become a fellow citizen, fighting in the army and voting in the Assembly beside the older man. They would then no longer be lovers, because sex between grown men was thought a little absurd in Athens. In Sparta, predictably, pederasty was a rougher, compulsory affair. Only in Thebes was adult homosexuality fully accepted, being epitomized in the 'Sacred Band', the elite corps of 300 lovers.

However, affections could long persist, most notably in Sparta but also in Athens. The reformer Solon when young loved the teenaged Pisistratus. Years later, when Pisistratus had become tyrant, he ignored his aged ex-lover's loud criticisms of his regime for old time's sake.

Above: 2nd-century AD statue of Antinous, the youth loved by Hadrian, who was of reputed royal descent and so almost the emperor's social equal.

THE HETEROSEXUAL MAJORITY

Above: A stele commemorating marital affection. Monogamous marriage remained the bedrock of Greek society, whatever men did in their youth.

Below: A man and woman exchanging sexually significant glances. Heterosexual affairs between equals could be hard in classical Athens, as women were kept so secluded. From a red figure krater c.460BC.

Most men and women in ancient Greece were predominantly heterosexual, however. In Homer, *all* erotic passion is between men and women. *The Iliad* is the archetypal book of love and war – of love because, although war predominates, the Trojan War originates in Paris' love for Helen. The epic itself starts with Achilles and Agamemnon quarrelling over Briseis, a slave girl. In *The Odyssey* Odysseus on his wanderings has many affairs with women, divine and human – the shipwrecking sirens who lure him so strongly are prototypical *femmes fatales* – before returning to his ever-faithful wife Penelope. Connubial affection rather than erotic passion marks their reunion in the marriage bed, but then neither is young.

In classical Athens Pericles lived for years with Aspasia, his mistress. He enjoyed her company not just in the bedroom but also at symposia, where she entertained Athens' best minds. While Pericles and Aspasia were exceptional, the comic playwright Aristophanes often voiced the feelings – erotic and political – of the Athenian man-in-the-street.

LESBIANISM: A HIDDEN LOVE

While the male half of the population was amusing itself with hetaerae or each other, Greek women cloistered in small, dark houses sought what consolations they could. Sex with another man was so risky that they presumably turned at times to each other. Their love has remained unrecorded except for Sappho, whose incandescently lyrical poetry has immortalized her passions. In Sparta, where women paradoxically enjoyed considerably more freedom, often exercising half naked, lesbianism was almost openly accepted.

WIVES ON STRIKE

In *Lysistrata*, one of Aristophanes' typically outrageous plays, staged in 411BC, the women of Athens, tired of the endless Peloponnesian war, follow Lysistrata's advice. They organize a sex-strike, denying their husbands their beds until the men agree to make peace. The strike is exported to Sparta and Thebes, Athens' enemies. The women have to seize the Acropolis and treasury to make the strike effective, but Sparta's ambassadors arrive with tales of similar strike action by their wives – and their own similar frustration. If Greek husbands never enjoyed having sex with their wives, the comedy would have lacked all point. But heterosexuality also found many extramarital outlets.

COURTESANS AND PROSTITUTES

Aspasia was originally a *hetaera*, a word meaning (female) 'companion'. In a notoriously misogynistic speech *Against Neaera*, Apollodorus in *c.*340BC said: "We have *hetaerae* for pleasure, *pallakae* (concubines) for physical needs and *gynaekes* (wives) to bear us legitimate children and be faithful guardians of our households."

This neat division of womankind into three types owed more to Apollodorus' wish to pigeonhole women than to social reality. While married women were distinct from hetaerae, prostitutes ranged from glamorous courtesans to '2-obol' streetwalkers, 2 obols being a third of a workman's daily wage. Grand hetaerae, who might became great men's lovers, charged hundreds of drachmae not for specific sexual acts but for their 'company'– hence their name. They also retained the crucial right to refuse anyone, so retaining some independence.

For those at the bottom of the scale, things were starkly different. The Kerameikos quarter was a red-light district notorious for streetwalkers of both sexes. These could be brutally treated, for the streets of Athens at night, unlit and unpoliced, were dangerous. The fate of prostitutes locked up in brothels was little better, however, for they were often foreign slaves, perhaps speaking only a little or no Greek.

GRAND HETAERAE

Neaera was in fact an expensive hetaera from Corinth, a city famous for its prostitutes, but she was also originally a slave, bought by two former clients. She was not, therefore, exactly the independent, cultured lady that romantic historians once thought. But the orator Lysias had his hetaera initiated at Eleusis, obviously caring for his lover's (assumed) fate in the next world too.

Thais, an Athenian hetaera, accompanied Ptolemy, one of Alexander's generals, on the conquest of Persia. At a banquet after the capture of Persepolis, she demanded the Persian capital be torched in revenge for the Persians burning Athens 150 years earlier. Persepolis duly went up in flames. The episode reveals that when courtesans attended wild Macedonian symposia, their voices were at times heeded. Later Ptolemy, on becoming king of Egypt, settled Thais and their three children comfortably. Then he married someone dynastically suitable.

Above: A man caressing a woman playing a lyre, probably a professional entertainer who sold sexual favours with her music. From a red figure cup of c.510BC.

Left: A 19th-century statue by Claude Rame of Sappho, the supreme women poet who was reputedly 'Lesbian' in the modern sense. Lesbianism presumably flourished unrecorded.

FOOD AND WINE

Above: Ritual sacrifice of animals, such as this pig, followed by a democratic public banquet, gave poorer Greeks their best chance of eating meat. From a red figure vase of c.500BC.

Below: Seafood always supplemented meat across Greece, as this fresco from Thira of c.1550BC attests. Fish was seldom particularly cheap, however.

The ancient Greeks could never be accused of being gourmands or gluttons. Even among the rich, food usually remained simple to the point of repetitive frugality. The Greek diet, focusing on olive oil, bread, fish and vegetables, appears at first glance like the precursor of the Mediterranean diet so recommended today. In fact it was far plainer, being a product of general poverty, not health-consciousness.

However, the Greeks compensated for their gastronomic austerity by being enthusiastic, even excessive, drinkers. Greek wines were valued around the Mediterranean not only by the Greeks but by Etruscans and later the Romans of the imperial period. This has led some historians to the suspicion that either tastes or Greek wine-making must have changed considerably since then.

DIETARY STAPLES

Although Greeks ate more than "a sort of porridge followed by another sort of porridge", in the words of one unimpressed reseacher, their diet was based on cereals. Bread was made from wheat when they could get it or afford it, and from barley or millet when they could not. Olives and olive oil, along with cheese – from sheep and especially goats, far more often than cows – pulses, beans and vegetables such as cabbage, onions and garlic supplemented bread.

A thick soup made chiefly from beans and lentils was a standard Greek dish. The Spartans, as ever unique, lived mostly off a 'black broth' reputedly made partly from blood and so disgusting that other Greeks gagged on it. Before setting off on their military expeditions, large quantities of this repellent mixture would be mixed up and carried by helots, to give their masters the consolation of home cooking while in foreign parts.

Fruits, including apples, plums, figs and grapes, were eaten, fresh in season and dried out of season. Sugar was unknown, honey being the only sweetener. Also unknown in the ancient world were rice, potatoes, tomatoes, (bell) peppers, citrus fruits, bananas, chocolate and many other now common fruits and vegetables, since introduced from around the world.

THE LUXURY OF MEAT

Meat was a luxury enjoyed by most Greeks only following the public sacrifice of a chicken, sheep, pig or bull. The priest would, after killing the animal, butcher it, removing the thigh bones and covering them with a little fat that was burned on the altar as an offering to the god invoked. While gods were deemed content with the mere smell of the beast, their human worshippers tucked into a communal feast eaten in the open. The meat was grilled (broiled) or boiled in cauldrons, each portion being conspicuously fair.

Little meat found its way to the market except for pork. This was relatively inexpensive, a suckling pig costing about three drachmae or three days' average wages. Some pork was also made into sausages. (Homer's heroes ate meat daily, but then they were really superhumans and not to be judged by normal standards in any way.) Athletes, especially those taking part in 'heavy' sports such as the pentathlon, might occasionally be put on a high-protein diet, even eating meat on a daily basis.

Fish was a useful supplement to the Greek diet, some species being much prized. Exactly what types of fish ancient names refer to is not always known. But fish too was relatively expensive, and not part of most people's daily diets. Nor was game, which, like fish, was never sacrificed. Interestingly, the Pythagoreans, almost the only vegetarians in the ancient

world, especially avoided fish, while they occasionally would eat sacrificed meat to conform to a polis' religious customs.

In classical Athens most shopping for food was done by men. This might seem strange in a male-dominated society where cooking and food had such a low status, but it followed, logically enough, from women's seclusion. Cooking was a different matter, however. There were no celebrity chefs in the Greek world. Instead, anonymous slaves and/or women cooked in small dark kitchens. Over open fires, meat was boiled or grilled, cooking being generally very simple.

WINES FAMOUS AND ORDINARY

Wine was drunk by Greeks wherever they lived – indeed, it was a mark of a true Hellene that he drank wine rather than beer, a drink fit only for barbarians. Wherever Greeks settled, they planted vines, and in so doing spread viticulture from the Black Sea to Gaul. (Tea, coffee and other non-alcoholic drinks were unknown, as were spirits.) Wine was strong, probably around 15 per cent alcohol, but was universally diluted, so that it would be no stronger than beer is today.

The Greeks recognized three colours of wine: 'black', 'white' and 'amber' (*kirrhos*). White and amber wines could be sweet or dry, black wines could be dry or 'medium'. Most wines were drunk young and rough, with half-fermented pieces of grape floating in them. Such wines would have tasted strongly of wineskins or resinated barrels.

The best wines came from Chios, Lesbos, Thasos and Mende in the Chalcidice in the north. They were bottled in distinctive clay amphorae, sealed airtight, that have been found around the Greek world. Although classical Greeks did not date wines by vintage – unlike the Mycenaeans and Romans – they understood the need to age the best wine.

Above: Families did, if rarely, eat together for festivals such as weddings, as this relief from Cyzicus on the Sea of Marmara of the 3rd century BC shows.

Below: Grapes and wine were always vital parts of the sparse Greek diet. This sarcophagus from Alexandria shows a grape harvest.

CITIZENS AND FOREIGNERS

Above: In 451BC Pericles introduced a law restricting Athenian citizenship to those with two full Athenian parents. This showed the value Athenians put on their citizenship but would have excluded Themistocles, the strategist behind victory at Salamis, whose mother was not Athenian.

Below: Ostraka (pot shards) with the name of Aristides, the politician ostracized in 482BC for opposing Themistocles' naval policy. Ostracism provided a useful safety valve.

In 451BC Pericles introduced a law that restricted Athenian citizenship to those with two full Athenian parents. This measure, meant partly to encourage Athenian colonists to wed Athenian women, would have disenfranchised Themistocles, Athens' saviour in the Persian wars, who had a non-Athenian mother. The law reveals the high value placed on citizenship by the classical polis.

Although we translate polis as city-state, 'citizen-state' would be a closer description, for a polis consisted of its citizens. (The word 'politics' comes from this Greek root.) Citizenship could be restricted under oligarchies. In Sparta, only the Equals, who had helots to till their land for them, counted as full Spartiates. (Their number, originally set at around 8,000, had declined to only 1,500 in the 4th century BC.) More numerous were the *perioeci* ('dwellers-around'), who lacked a Spartiate's rights and obligations but provided much of the army and revenue.

In Athens after Solon's reforms in 594BC, all free men ranked as citizens, despite the poorest being excluded from important posts until the 5th century BC. By 432BC there were *c*.60,000 adult male citizens in Attica, although plague and war soon reduced their number. In 404BC the junta of the Thirty Tyrants restricted citizenship to the 3,000 richest citizens, but the revived democracy at once restored the full franchise.

DUTIES AND PRIVILEGES

The most demanding duty for an adult Athenian citizen was military service, which he had to undertake at any age between 18 and 61. Although Athens' hoplite army remained amateur and part-time compared to Sparta's – and later to Thebes' – military service was a recurrent, often dangerous burden. In contrast, the

Above: An Athenian citizen-soldier saying goodbye to his family, from an Attic vase of c.440BC. Military service was demanded of every citizen between the ages of 18 and 61.

Athenian fleet of *c*.300 triremes rowed by the *thetes*, free but poor citizens, rapidly became a semi-professional force after the Persian war. However triremes were usually laid up in winter.

Citizens also had to serve on the huge juries, typically 501 men strong, selected by lot from a roster of 6,000 men. At least once in their lives most also served on the Council of 500. Modest pay for these offices – as for fighting in the fleet or army – was introduced in the 5th century, but was no more an inducement for an able-bodied citizen than jury pay is today. Richer citizens also faced the extra burdens and honours of the *liturgies*, such as the choreogia (the financing and staging of plays).

Although the Athenian state had no real welfare system, it did provide modest support for the arts. By the 4th century BC, free tickets for the theatre, the greatest public entertainment and an occasion for the whole polis to manifest its collective identity, were available for poorer citizens. The orphans of citizens killed fighting for Athens also received state support as children.

METICS: TRADING PLACES

Foreign-born permanent residents of Athens were known as metics (*metoikoi*), meaning literally those who have changed their home. After the Persian wars (499–478BC), many Greeks from Ionia migrated to Athens to make their living. They had to pay a special poll tax (*metoikon*) of one drachma per month, as well as normal taxes. Failure to pay the metoikon promptly could mean enslavement.

While metics were liable for military service, they were not allowed to vote or hold office. Nor could they own land – a severe disadvantage in a society where land was still the safest form of wealth. They had, however, access to the courts, although they had to post bail, unlike citizens. Occasionally, citizenship, or citizen rights, were granted to exceptionally worthy metics such as Pasion. In 338BC, after Athens' defeat by Macedonia, it was proposed to enfranchise all metics to boost the citizen body, but the measure was not carried out.

Despite their disadvantages, the number of metics in Athens grew rapidly in the 5th century, reaching about 20,000 men by 431BC. These metics lived mainly in the Piraeus, where they played leading roles in commerce and banking. Many distinguished, wealthy men, including the shield-maker Cephalus, the philosopher Aristotle and the orator Lysias, were metics. Lysias had strongly supported the exiled democrats in 404BC. Granted citizenship at their triumph, he made cogent speeches before being disenfranchised again by the grudging Athenian demos.

The Roman emperor Claudius (reigned AD41–54) later compared Greek cities' parsimony in granting citizenship with Rome's generosity. This winning of conquered people's acquiescence and often their active support was seen as a secret of Rome's imperial success. But a Greek polis was inherently a small, autonomous unit in which citizens took active part. Roman citizens, by contrast, fought but seldom voted for their city, as Rome's empire grew. By AD212, when Caracalla gave all free men Roman citizenship, it had lost much of its value anyway.

Right: Marble bust of Lysias (c.455–380BC), a metic who was made a citizen for his services to democracy, only to be later demoted again.

Below: A cobbler, either a poorer citizen or a metic (a resident foreigner). From a black figure vase of the early 5th century BC.

SLAVERY
FACTS AND MYTHS

Above: A shaft in a silver mine at Laurium, where Greek slavery was at its worst. Tens of thousands of slaves worked and died there in appalling conditions that no free man would have accepted but which almost no one at the time condemned.

Greek civilization depended on slavery. This fact – which is indisputable but one that has made many Greek scholars uncomfortable – can mislead. To begin with, slavery in antiquity had no racial connotations. Although most slaves were foreign-born in the Classical period, Greeks themselves always risked being enslaved if they were captured. The Cynic sage Diogenes – and even Plato reputedly – suffered this philosophy-testing fate, although both were soon freed.

The Greeks did not pioneer what has been called 'chattel slavery', meaning buying and selling enslaved persons as objects. It was already common among other seafaring peoples like the Carthaginians and Phoenicians, while absolute monarchies such as Persia, Egypt and Babylon had long been accustomed to controlling vast armies of slaves.

Right: A man using a strigil (scraper) after exercising while his slave boy holds a jar of olive oil for him, c.400BC. Most slavery in classical Greece was small-scale. Many slaves came from the Black Sea area or Asia Minor, often being sold as children. War was another source of slaves, for captured cities' inhabitants were normally enslaved.

Nor did owning slaves make most Greeks rich, for slavery in the Greek world was normally small-scale. Slaves were, like cars today, generally thought of as useful, even essential, to everyday life.

Slaves worked in the house or workshop or on the farm alongside free labourers. Contrary to myth, slaves almost never rowed Athens' or other cities' galleys, a job done by poor citizens – who wanted the modest wages, and became highly professional oarsmen. (In the Hellenistic era, when fleets and ships grew massively larger, slaves were at times used.) Nor did slaves labour in great gangs on large estates. Most Greek farms were tiny.

An unskilled slave cost c.200 drachmae (a drachma was a skilled worker's daily wage) and the same to clothe and feed each year. Demosthenes, whose wealthy father had owned skilled metal-worker slaves, said each cost 500–600 drachmae. Neaera, the beautiful slave-prostitute, cost 3,000 drachmae, but she was exceptional. There was very seldom a quick profit to be made in owning a slave.

As most Greeks strongly disliked working for their fellow citizens, slave labour could be easier than employing free men. Slaves and free men worked side by side in small groups building the Acropolis temples, doing exactly the same work in the same conditions. The difference, of course, was that the free workers kept their modest pay while the slave workers saw it all go to their masters.

ASPECTS OF SLAVERY

The numbers of slaves in Athens, the best-documented as well as richest city, is estimated at c.80,000–100,000 in 431BC, about 25 per cent of the population. Most were in domestic service. The affluent Aristotle, who defended slavery, had 18 household slaves. More typical, however, is the disabled citizen for whom Lysias

made a speech claiming public support. He claimed his client was too ill to work himself but not yet able to buy a slave to work for him.

Female slaves worked in the house as servants and nurses, some becoming almost part of the family. However, they had no redress against their masters beating or sexually abusing them, although killing slaves was a crime. When slaves were witnesses in legal cases, they were routinely tortured first. Otherwise it was thought they would never dare testify against their masters.

Skilled male slaves were often set up in their own workshops. This was called 'living apart' and some earned enough extra money at their trade to buy their freedom. Freedmen had the same limited rights as metics. Pasion, a freedman probably born in Syria, became a rich banker and manufacturer – using slaves – in the 4th century BC. For donating armaments to Athens during a crisis, he was granted citizenship, a rare honour for anyone.

Pasion was exceptional, however. The real feelings of most Athenian slaves were shown by how many ran away to Deceleia, the fort occupied by the Spartans after 413BC: 20,000, according to Thucydides. Although the nearest source of slaves was Greek war-captives, growing demand meant that slaves came from many areas. The Balkans, Asia Minor, Syria and the Black Sea were prime sources. These slaves often came through trade, not raids or conquest, i.e. other peoples sold the Greeks slaves, including often their own children.

HELOTS: SPARTA'S SERFS
Sparta, as always distinctive, had its own form of slaves in the helots, native Greeks of Messenia. Their forebears had been enslaved by Spartan conquest and they were tied to the land they cultivated, i.e. they could not be bought or sold, unlike slaves in Corinth or Athens. Although sometimes called serfs, helots were as unfree as any slaves. But, retaining their national identity, they were unusually prone to revolt. Spartans, Xenophon noted, always went around fully armed because of this threat. Every year Sparta formally declared war against the helots, allowing possible ringleaders to be murdered. Yet at times helots fought bravely for Sparta even abroad – for example under Brasidas in 424BC.

MINES: INFERNAL LABOUR
One form of slavery stands out for its sheer horror: the mines. Slave labour was the norm here, for few free men would work underground in poor conditions. About 20,000 slaves were employed at the peak of the silver mines at Laurium, revenues from which underpinned Athenian power. Nicias, the politician who led the Syracusan expedition to disaster, owned 1,000 slaves at Laurium, a fact not thought remotely shocking at the time. Slaves also laboured in the gold mines at Mt Pangaeus in Macedonia.

During the Hellenistic and Roman periods, slaves – including children who were small enough to crawl through very low tunnels – were employed in Egypt's gold mines on a massive scale. Many were literally worked to death underground, where tiny skeletons have been found.

Left: Bust of Aristotle, who defended slavery, saying some men were born so naturally brutish they were better off belonging to a master. He practised what he preached, finally owning 18 domestic slaves.

Below: Neaera, an exceptionally beautiful slave-prostitute from Corinth, as pictured by the Victorian artist H.J. Hudson. She cost 3,000 drachmae but most slaves were much cheaper.

WOMEN
A VARYING STATUS

Above: Women, left on their own as their men went out into the city, turned to entertaining themselves, here making music. In Plato's Symposium *it was suggested that the auletris, the female flute-player, should go upstairs to entertain the house's women.*

The traditional picture of Greek women is bleak. Excluded from politics and culture, never owning property in their own right, always dependent on a male relative, they seem hardly freer than slaves.

Aristotle's generally misgoynistic views provided intellectual support for female subordination. Women were, he thought, too emotional and passionate to act rationally, even if they could *think* clearly. Even their role in child bearing was only as passive receptacles for male seed. If his views reveal women's oppressed status in classical Athens, the fate of women elsewhere in Greece possibly differed markedly over the centuries. It appears, though firm evidence is lacking, that other Greek women at times had far more freedom.

MINOANS TO MACEDONIANS

In Minoan Crete women probably played a prominent role in religious and social life. Whether they had any political power is unknown, although the idea of a matriarchy is implausible. Mycenaean Greece was a militaristic society, but its women were probably not cloistered away. The prominent role of women in myth and tragedy may reflect memories of their Bronze Age importance.

In Homer, women have significant roles. In *The Iliad* Helen is less condemned for her adultery than admired for her imperilling beauty. In *The Odyssey* women are often active players: Calypso the nymph entraps Odysseus while the princess Nausicaa helps his final return. However, the patient cunning of Penelope, epitomized by her unravelling the tapestry she has woven every night to put off suitors wanting her hand and fortune, was probably far more typical of a woman's role.

In the Archaic Age (700–500BC) Sappho enjoyed enough freedom to write and love, traditionally setting up her own female academy in Lesbos. As she went into exile for a while, she presumably had an active interest in politics too. In Sparta, women always enjoyed unusual freedom. To help produce tough soldier-sons, they exercised half-naked, shocking if fascinating other Greeks. By the 4th century BC they could inherit land and choose husbands, with disastrous consequences, as wealth became concentrated in ever fewer hands. In Doric Crete, culturally half-Spartan, women in Gortyna could inherit half their brothers' share of land.

Left: A Maenad dancing to flute music. The orgiastic rites of Dionysus, celebrated outside the city, gave some women a rare break from their usual life of domestic drudgery. From a red figure kylix of c.510BC.

In Macedonia, still half-reminiscent of the Homeric world, women at times had crucial roles. Olympias, Alexander's tempestuous mother, had furious rows with her husband Philip, going into exile once. After Alexander's death, she became a major player in dynastic politics. In the Hellenistic age, queens at times ruled, the most famous monarch being Cleopatra VII of Egypt (69–30BC), who tried to revive Ptolemaic power through her affair with Mark Antony, the Roman general.

SECLUSION IN ATHENS

In Athens, women could hope for no such potential glory. Married off young, at best half-educated, women in theory had to content themselves with domestic duties in their houses. This included weaving, for most clothes were home-made – even Penelope, queen of Ithaca, wove. (Poorer women had to work in the fields or in shops as well.)

As men or slaves did most shopping, women's best chance to socialize was collecting water from the fountains, as private water supplies were almost unknown. Even this was denied rich women, whose slaves fetched the water.

Respectable women did not attend symposia. Only flute girls, dancers and prostitutes entered the andron, the men's room. Instead, women were restricted to the gynaeikon, their rooms upstairs. But they may at times have been entertained there. In Plato's *Symposium* it was suggested that the *auletris*, the (female) flute-player, should go upstairs and entertain the women. Women also seem to have attended the theatre after *c.*400BC; some are reported to have fainted at alarming performances. This exception to their seclusion emphasizes their high status as Athenian citizens, albeit unenfranchised female ones.

PRIESTESSES AND MAENADS

In one area women played a decisive role even in Athens: religion. The patron deity of the city was the goddess Athena, served by priestesses. In the great Panathenaea

Right: A vase from Apulia of 340BC showing Penelope, Odysseus' faithful wife, spinning wool.

every July, four nobly born maidens, the *arrephoroi*, led the procession. Other goddesses also had their own priestesses, especially Artemis, whose sanctuary at Brauron had female acolytes.

Some festivals were for women only. Men were excluded from the *Thesmophoria*, a major three-day festival throughout Greece. Celebrated in the autumn to honour Demeter, goddess of agriculture, the rites culminated in the sacrifice of a pig.

Another, far more thrilling, god offered women intoxicating release from their daily grind: Dionysus, god of wine and drama. His ecstatic rites took place in March outside the city, when women, drunk on wine and the god, went raving mad – the literal meaning of 'Maenad' – as they roamed the country-side. Men avoided these rites for their lives' sake.

Below: Preparations for a marriage, giving a relatively rare glimpse into domestic life. From a red figure vase of c.470BC.

FAMILY AND MARRIAGE

Women never legally came of age in classical Athens or in most other Greek cities. This meant that they always remained wards of their *kyrios* (master/lord), who might be their father, their uncle, brother or, of course, their husband. Woman could never control or own any property, nor could they choose their husband.

A girl, who would have spent her life inside her home, was betrothed, often as young as 5, and married around the age of 14 or 15 to a man, selected by her family, usually twice her age.

The overriding concern in Greece was the continuation of the family line, not a girl's happiness. Women's prime role in life was seen as producing children, as men's was fighting for the polis.

Xenophon, the historian and general, wrote: "My bride would have known nothing of how I lived, for until she entered my house she had had a very restricted life, trained from childhood … to ask no unnecessary questions." A wife then saw her husband only in private, his social, political and intellectual life being barred to her – at least in theory. In practice, relations between the sexes were often happier, Greek fathers being as fond of their children as any others. But Socrates was not that unusual in dismissing his family to debate with his friends before his death.

MARRIAGE AND WEDDINGS

In Athens wedding festivities lasted three days. At the betrothal (*egge*, pledge) the groom formally accepted his bride, who was given away by her kyrios with the words: "I give you this woman for the begetting of legitimate children."

The wedding itself was often set for the day of the full moon. Celebrations started on the day before, when sacrifices were made to varied gods, including Artemis, goddess of virginity, Hera, goddess of marriage and Aphrodite, the love-goddess. The bride then took a sad farewell of her childhood toys, offering them to the gods, while the women of her family fetched water in a torchlight procession from the Fountain of Callirhoe for her *loutron nymphikon*, ritual bath. She was then carefully dressed, with a special bridal veil. (This was, however, almost the only time Greek women wore veils.) The groom meanwhile had a similar bath. Olive and laurel branches adorned both houses as the groom, garlanded and anointed with myrrh, went with his relations and best man to the bride's house in the afternoon.

After sacrificing to the gods, they sat down to a banquet given by the bride's kyrios – one of the rare occasions women and men ate together in public, although they still sat separately. The traditional food included sesame seeds, symbolizing fertility, one of Persephone's attributes. Guests then gave the bride wedding presents and at night fall the kyrios formally presented the bride to the groom.

Bride and groom then went in a chariot amid a procession to her husband's house. An *amphithales*, a child with both parents

Above: A woman spinning with a distaff, spindle and whorl, typical activities expected of a housewife. From a lekythos (white background vase) of c.490BC.

Below: A wedding procession with the bride and groom in the chariot and Eros, god of desire, hovering overhead. From a red figure pyxis of the 5th century BC.

still alive, escorted the bride. He represented prosperity and good luck for the couple and their expected children. The bride carried a sieve and a grill, symbolizing her coming domestic duties. On arrival, the crowd threw nuts and dried figs at the happy couple, who then retired to their bedchamber. Outside, the groom's friends sang marriage hymns lustily. The next day, the bride's parents or other relatives brought their gifts and the dowry to the couple in their new home. Then the door closed on a wife's life of domestic drudgery.

SPARTAN CUSTOMS

In Sparta, they organized things differently. The bride had her hair hacked off, she was dressed in a boy's short tunic, and her husband pretended to rape her. Such sexual violence was thought to help beget warriors. For the first years of marriage a husband could only slip away from his barracks at night to visit his wife secretly. Only later could couples properly set up house together.

Despite this, and perhaps because of the consequent fall in birth rate, a Spartan woman may have led a freer life than her Athenian counterpart, who bore an estimated nine children during her life.

INFANTICIDE

As the Greeks had no contraception and abortion was dangerous, the chief form of birth control was infanticide. Killing one's child was illegal in Athens, but a father could reject a child because it was an unwanted daughter or because it was sickly. (In Sparta the state decided which children should live.) The child was then exposed on a hill outside the city. Sometimes such babies were rescued by childless women and brought up as their own, but most of them died. The classical polis would have been surrounded by the tiny skeletons of such abandoned infants. It was a hard world.

Above: Callicrate and her daughters, one playing with a tortoise. From a relief at Smyrna of the Hellenistic era.

Left: Mother and child, a fine funerary relief from classical Athens. Women's quiet efforts were perhaps sometimes appreciated only after their deaths, although many couples were presumably devoted to each other.

CHILDHOOD AND EDUCATION

Greek education aimed to produce soldiers for the citizen-armies, and for a select minority, orators for public life. For most Greeks education was limited to the three Rs. Music mattered, but physical education in the gymnasium was what counted for most. For a fortunate few, however, education higher than anything known before developed during the later 5th century BC.

FIRST STEPS

About a week after a baby's birth it was formally accepted in a ritual cleansing, the *amphidromia*, followed by a banquet. Richer mothers had wet-nurses and nannies to look after their infants. Children learnt fairy tales from Aesop's fables, as Socrates recalled in his death cell.

Elementary education was not compulsory, being private and fee-paying if inexpensive. From the age of six, most boys attended three types of school: one for gymnastics, under a *paidotribes* (physical trainer); one for music and poetry under a *kitharistes* (lyre player), for poetry was often accompanied by music; and one for the three Rs under a *grammatistes* (school teacher). Homer was the great authority whose poems every boy learnt by heart. There were no desks, boys sitting on stools using wood-backed wax writing tablets and a stylus of bone or metal. Papyrus, paper's precursor, was very expensive.

Many boys had a *paidagogos*, a slave tutor to teach them good manners and punish them if they misbehaved. Meanwhile, girls from wealthier families were taught at home to read, write and play the lyre. Most teachers were slaves or underpaid freedmen. The exception was the paidotribes, a stern-looking figure with cloak and stick, who supervised boys' exercises in the gymnasium or palaestra (wrestling-ground), who was well paid. In the Hellenistic cities scattered across Asia, gymnasia were far more than just gyms, being social and cultural beacons of Hellenism. Libraries now also became important for scholars.

Above: A baby crawling, on a vase painting from c.400BC. Such family scenes were pictured in classical Athens.

Below: A terracotta figurine of a schoolboy, from c.300BC from the Lebanon, by then a Hellenized region.

THE FIRST UNIVERSITIES

On his return to Athens around 387BC after years of travel, Plato founded what became the first university. He chose an olive grove sacred to the hero Academus. It stood nearly a mile (1.6km) from Athens, outside the city that had executed Socrates but would tolerate his own muted yet more radical criticisms of it. The curriculum included mathematics, dialectic and political theory. Despite his belief in an ideal world, Plato intended to train philosopher-rulers for this world. But only one graduate, Dion of Syracuse, ever had real power, and his career proved disastrous. Plato headed the Academy for 40 years, his nephew Speusippus succeeding him. After a period dominated by the Sceptics, the Academy returned to Platonism in the 1st century BC. It later became a beacon of Neoplatonism, surviving until AD529, when it was closed by imperial decree. Aristotle, the Academy's most brilliant student, founded his own school, the Lyceum, in 334BC. Modelled on the Academy, with similar common meals and symposia, it was less exclusive and less anti-democratic. Systematic large-scale scientific research began in the Lyceum's large library and collections. After Aristotle's death, this encyclopaedic approach was neglected in favour of narrower philosophical studies. Rhodes, Pergamum and Alexandria later offered places of similar higher education.

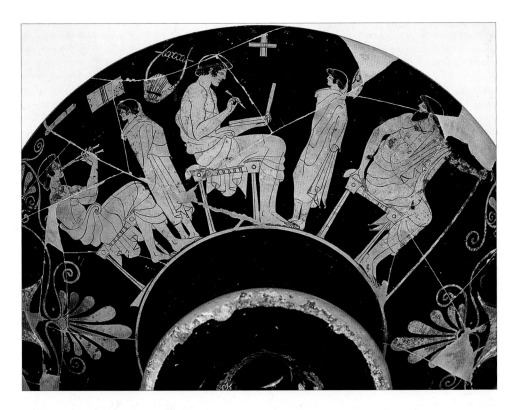

RHETORIC: AN AMBIVALENT GIFT

At the age of 12, the sons of wealthier men went to secondary schools offering courses in law, rhetoric or medicine. Then for two years, from the age of 18, ephebes did military training, although this appears to have become institutionalized only in the 4th century BC. For the politically ambitious, being able to speak well, to sway the Assembly or lawcourts, was vital. Rhetoric, the art of speech-making, was the glamorous new way to attain the gift of the gab.

The main teachers of rhetoric in the 5th century BC were Sophists (literally, wise men). Some were unscrupulous spin-doctors, but the best, including Protagoras and Gorgias, were profound thinkers. Isocrates (436–338BC), a notably prolific writer – or windbag – embodied the worst excesses of rhetoric.

The finest rhetorician was Demosthenes of Athens (384–322BC). Reputedly afflicted with a bad stammer when young, he cured himself, later delivering some of the most impassioned if ineffectual speeches in democratic history. Rhetoric became a revered subject –

Aristotle wrote a whole book on it – being widely taught under Roman rule, despite democracy's demise. A chair in rhetoric was even established in the new university of Constantinople, the Byzantine capital, in AD425.

THE SPARTAN EXCEPTION

In education the Spartans had their own special *agoge*, or upbringing. Boys, taken from their mothers at the age of seven, were for ten years brought up in singularly brutal boarding schools run by older boys. Institutionalized pederasty was the norm there. Dancing and singing were taught but were subordinate to overall physical toughening and testing.

This training included survival techniques such as having to steal their daily food and being savagely whipped if caught. With it went the regimentation that made Spartans both feared and mocked. From the age of 20 to 30, men lived in barracks undergoing yet further military training.

CLOTHING AND HAIRSTYLES

Above: Minoan women curled their hair and wore colourful dresses, typical of their cheerful culture, which was so different to later Greek severity.

The Greeks were never the slaves of fashion. Indeed at first glance their clothing seems to have remained unchanged over centuries. But styles did alter slowly, becoming simpler at the beginning of the Classical period and a bit more luxurious – for those who could afford it – in the Hellenistic Age. But the chief characteristic of Greek dress was its simplicity.

Minoan and Mycenaean styles differed radically from later fashions. Women in Crete wore long, elaborately flounced dresses, nipped in at the waist with little jackets that often left their breasts bare. Men went naked to the waist, with tightly belted kilts. Mycenaean women copied Minoan styles, but men usually wore breeches or shorts and tunics. Both sexes wore jewellery. The collapse of these palace-based civilizations after 1200BC meant the end of luxurious styles. Clothes became far simpler as classical Greek clothing emerged over the centuries.

THE MALE ESSENTIALS

Free men wore a loose-fitting tunic (*chiton*) made of wool or sometimes linen, fastened at both shoulders and tied at the waist. A young man's chiton reached to his knees, an older man's to his ankles. Over the chiton they often wrapped a cloak (*himation*), a large rectangular piece of cloth draped over the left shoulder with the back brought round under the right arm. Surplus material hanging down over the body could be gathered up in cold weather. The *chlamys*, a short cloak or cape, was worn for hunting or riding and by soldiers. Draped around the shoulders, it was fastened at the throat with a clasp,

Above: A koure (girl) showing her hair elaborately braided and wearing an ornate multi-coloured dress in the Archaic style. An Athenian statue of c.530BC.

for the Greeks did not use buttons, a much later invention. Nor did they wear underclothes of any sort. Men normally went bare-headed, but a wide felt or straw hat, the *petasos*, was worn at times by travellers and hunters, and a skull cap, the *pilos*, by labourers. The Macedonians were especially noted for wearing the petasos.

Labourers and slaves wore a single garment fastened over the left shoulder, the *exomis*, or in hot weather simply a loin cloth (*zoma*). Athletes, of course, competed and exercised naked.

Left: Women's hairstyles and clothes became far simpler at the beginning of the Classical Age (c.480BC). From then on, fashion changed only marginally over a long period.

Footwear was simple for both sexes and all classes, consisting of sandals of varying types, often no more than a sole with two or three straps. In winter, sturdier laced-up boots were sometimes worn but socks were unknown.

WOMEN'S CLOTHES

Female fashions were also simple and changed very slowly. In the Archaic period, women at times wore elaborate multi-coloured dresses, but by 500BC these had given way to the Doric style of dress, far closer to men's clothing. It consisted of a plain long woollen or linen chiton held by two pins at the shoulder and falling to their ankles. Some variety was introduced by sleeves being gathered at different points, creating pleats. The himation was draped over the tunic in much the same way as men's but could be wrapped around the whole head and body so that only the eyes were visible.

Women are often shown with bare feet on vases, but this was probably a convention or depicted them at home.

Silk from China became known after Alexander's conquests but remained very expensive, worn only by great queens such as Cleopatra. Cheaper but coarser was 'wild silk' from the island of Cos.

HAIR AND BEARDS

Down to the late 6th century BC, Greek men usually wore their hair long. A sign of the advent of Classicism, typified by the *Critios Boy* of *c*.480BC, was the adoption of shorter hair by men, although the Spartans were as always slow to change. This trend was not universal. Some gods and priests were still shown with long hair in the 5th century, as were some heroes. By the 4th century BC almost all men wore their hair short, but Alexander wore his romantically long.

Minoan men seem to have been clean-shaven, but Mycenaeans always wore beards. So did all adult Greek men right down to about 350BC. Then a fashion, started by the sculptors Praxiteles and Lysippus for showing men clean-shaven, was adopted enthusiastically by Alexander and his successors. From then on, men were clean-shaven, apart from philosophers and seers. This style was emulated by the Romans until Hadrian.

Women always had long hair, often pulled back in a ponytail or a bun and fastened by ribbons, or tied in elaborate patterns. Sometimes hair was artificially curled, judging by vase paintings. Head scarves of various types and colours were popular, allowing flashes of decoration.

Above: On the frieze of the Parthenon, carved under the direction of the master-sculptor Pheidias, the calm, timeless simplicity of Classical clothing is apparent for both men's and women's clothes.

Below: In the Archaic period (c.700–480BC) men's hair and even beards were often tightly curled, as this Athenian statue shows.

THE END AND REBIRTH OF ANCIENT GREECE

In 146BC the Roman general Lucius Mummius sacked Corinth, totally destroying the city and enslaving its inhabitants. This act of exemplary brutality – one of many at the time, as Rome stamped its power across the Mediterranean world – marked the end of independence in Greece proper. Over the next 120 years the whole Hellenistic world west of the Euphrates passed under Roman sway, at times being dragged into Rome's ruinous civil wars. Mummius had taken great care, however, to have Corinth's finest artworks packed and shipped to Rome, where they were displayed to appreciative observers. His actions symbolize the dual-faced nature of Roman rule. This preserved, indeed even revived, Greek cultural life while crushing the Greeks' final hopes of regaining their political liberty.

ROME, GREECE'S CAPTIVE

The Romans by c.120BC had the greatest admiration for Greek culture but almost no regard at all for contemporary Greeks, whom they saw as frivolous, unworthy heirs of the great age of Pericles. One building epitomizes Rome's philhellenism at the time: the temple of Hercules Victor in the heart of Rome. Built c.120BC as a perfect circle with slim marble columns, it is supremely Greek in form, owing very little to native Italian tradition. Equally Greek in form and spirit are the wall paintings of Pompeii, which were probably made by actual Greek artists copying Hellenistic master-works. Horace, one of the greatest Latin poets, later wrote: "Greece made captive captured its conquerors and introduced the arts into backward Latium."

Greek culture transplanted remarkably well to Rome. It had shown it could thrive almost as much under monarchies as in democracies – from Pisistratus' enlightened tyranny in 6th-century BC Athens to the absolutism of Ptolemaic Egypt in the 3rd, when Alexandria's Museum/Library became the powerhouse of Hellenic culture. The Romans now showed a genius for absorbing, adapting and transmitting Greek culture across western Europe, albeit in vulgarized form. (The typical buildings of a Roman city were the amphitheatre, forum and public baths, not the theatre, library and gymnasium.)

PHILHELLENIC ROMANS

By the time of Cicero (106–43BC), almost every educated Roman spoke fluent Greek. Many, including Cicero, went to Greece to complete their education. (Few Greeks ever learnt much Latin, however.) Cicero, when he had a moment to spare from politics in the Republic's last years, translated and summarized Greek philosophy in books such as *De Finibus* (*Concerning Aims*) and *Republic*. In doing so he invented terms such as *moralis*, *qualitas*, *beatitudo* (moral, quality, happiness), still current today. Roman playwrights such as Plautus and Terence, poets such as Catullus, Virgil and Ovid and architects such as Vitruvius were all acutely aware of their debt to Greece.

Above: Athen's Temple of Olympian Zeus, finally completed after 600 years under the emperor Hadrian in c.130AD, epitomizes the Graeco-Roman synthesis.

Below: Greek cultural prestige was so strong across the Roman Empire that even Leptis Magna in Libya, a city with no Greek connections, began importing pentelic marble from Attica for its finest buildings.

Above: Roman statue of Cicero (106–43BC), who translated much Greek philosophy into Latin – a huge gain for a posterity in the medieval West after it had forgotten Greek.

Above: The well-preserved theatre of Sabratha in Roman Africa (Libya) reveals how Greek culture spread under the Pax Romana, *shaping life and art even in areas never previously Hellenized.*

Augustus, Rome's first emperor (reigned 30BC–AD14), was not as openly philhellenic as his defeated opponent Mark Antony, who had debated with philosophers in Athens and been hailed as Dionysus by Greeks in Alexandria. But, by establishing a lasting peace, Augustus allowed the Greek east to recover its wealth and, ultimately, its self-confidence. He ended being worshipped by Greeks as a saviour-god in gratitude.

The last of Augustus' dynasty, Nero (reigned AD54–68), went further, in effect trying to turn Rome into a Hellenistic kingdom. While Greeks might applaud acts of Neronian generosity such as granting Achaea (Greece proper) 'freedom' from taxes and starting the Corinth Canal, Romans, appalled by his extravagance, rebelled. Nero's reign ended in civil wars and was followed by a brief anti-Hellenic reaction.

THE ANTONINE SYNTHESIS
Under Hadrian (reigned AD117–38) and his Antonine successors, considered among Rome's finest emperors, the Greeks finally became Romans' social and political equals. Plutarch the biographer (AD46–125), whose grandfather as a boy had had to carry grain sacks across mountains to help feed Antony's troops, accepted imperial office as procurator of Achaea, although his heart remained in his native Chaeronea. More eloquently symbolic, the aristocratic Greek historian Arrian became a consul – the highest post in the empire after the emperor's – and then commanded a Roman army.

Hadrian himself became archon at Athens, ordering the completion of the vast Temple to Olympian Zeus begun 630 years earlier and being initiated into the Eleusinian Mysteries. He also had a very public affair with Antinous, a boy reputedly descended from Hellenized Bithynian kings, something which might be called truly Hellenic.

Right: The proudly imperial Prima Porta statue of Augustus, first Roman emperor, was based on Polyclitus' classical Diadomenus of 400 years earlier. The 'Classical Canon' was by then definitively established.

Above: The Neoplatonist philosopher-emperor Julian (reigned AD361–3), Rome's last non-Christian ruler, wanted to create an organized pagan religion to counter Christianity. But his reign ended in military disaster in Persia and he had no philhellenic successors.

Fifty years after Hadrian's reign, the philosopher-emperor Marcus Aurelius endowed four chairs of philosophy at Athens: the Platonist, Peripatetic (Aristotelian), Stoic and Epicurean. Marcus wrote his *Meditations* in Greek.

TWILIGHT OF THE GODS

A religion that satisfied people's varied needs as well as Graeco-Roman polytheism might have been expected to last indefinitely. Philosophical scepticism did not touch popular religion, which happily incorporated new gods such as Isis. Around AD250 the Olympic Games were still being held, sacrifices were still made to the Olympians and the Eleusinian Mysteries still promised initiates salvation in the afterworld. Urban decay did not harm a religion rooted in rural life.

Christianity could and did. After AD312 Christianity slowly became the officially favoured religion and then the only religion tolerated. Early Christians thought the pagan gods not charming myths but active malicious demons. Although at least 90 per cent of the population in AD312 was still pagan, Christians vehemently attacked the ancient cults, whose adherents lacked monotheists' fanaticism.

JULIAN, THE LAST PHILHELLENE

Rome's last non-Christian ruler, the philosopher-emperor Julian (reigned AD361–3), attempted to restore urban self-government, long decayed, and to create an organized pagan priesthood to counter Christianity. Although he refused actually to persecute Christians, he forbade them to teach Greek literature, the core of Graeco-Roman life. But Julian's reign ended in disaster in Persia and he had no philhellenic successors. In c.AD386 the fanatical Christian Theodosius I banned most pagan worship.

Even so, paganism was a long time dying. The cult of the healer-god Asclepius at Epidaurus thrived into the mid-5th century AD; a century later peasants in Asia Minor were still being converted en masse. In Athens the philosophy schools remained proudly Hellenic until closed in AD529. When the Byzantines reconquered the Peloponnese in c.AD830, they found peasants in remoter corners still worshipping Zeus.

HELLENISM REBORN

At the Councils of Ferrara and Florence in 1438, called to try to reunite the Catholic and Orthodox churches, the Greek philosopher Gemistus Plethon dazzled Westerners with his esoteric Neoplatonism. Bessarion, a more orthodox scholar, stayed on to rekindle knowledge of Greek in the West, where it had been forgotten. The fall of Constantinople in 1453 and the diaspora of Greek scholars fuelled Italian passion for things Greek. In 1462 the Academy was founded in Florence – its name deliberately recalling

Left: The Supreme Court in Washington DC shows the lasting influence of Graeco-Roman ideas. It was constructed in majestically Classical style in 1935.

Above: The rediscovery of truly Greek architecture in the later 18th century led to much simpler styles, such as that of the British Museum, London, built by Robert Smirke in 1823–46.

Plato's school – to study Greek literature and philosophy. It proved vastly influential, begetting similar bodies across Italy and inspiring artists such as Botticelli – whose *Birth of Venus* hides a Neoplatonist allegory – and Michelangelo. Michelangelo was moved by the spiritual anguish he discerned in the newly unearthed Laocoön group to create works on a gigantic scale, from his hopeful *David* to his overwhelming *Last Judgement* in the Sistine Chapel. When even Pope Leo X (reigned 1513–21) could celebrate the birthday of 'Saint Socrates', Hellenism was clearly resurrected and walking the streets of Italy.

By 1500 the passion for Greek culture had crossed the Alps. A chair in Divinity was founded at Cambridge University in England, Erasmus (1466–1536), the Dutch humanist and scholar, being among its first occupants. Erasmus had learnt Greek primarily to translate the New Testament. His new version revealed so many faults in the old Latin Bible that it helped trigger the Reformation. Protestantism and Platonism formed a fruitful synthesis at Cambridge. In the 17th century the scholars known as the 'Cambridge Platonists' found in Platonism a way of rebutting both fanatical Calvinism and Hobbesian reductionism.

REVIVALS AND REVOLUTIONS

The late 18th century saw a revolution in the arts as in politics. West Europeans returned from seeing at first hand the ruins of Greece (then under Turkish rule) with news of heroic, austere architecture and art. Superseding the impact of discoveries at Pompeii, this led to radically simpler fashions in art, architecture and even clothing. Jane Austen's heroines wore free-flowing 'Grecian' gowns.

This Greek revival led to a new appreciation of Hellenism, especially in Britain and Germany. The poet John Keats was overwhelmed on seeing the Elgin Marbles – carvings removed from the Parthenon by Lord Elgin, a deeply controversial act – as his poetry reveals. Almost the whole work of Shelley, his contemporary and a superb classicist, breathes Greek fire.

Some of Germany's finest poets, such as Goethe and Friedrich Hölderlin, were similarly moved. In the mid-19th century Richard Wagner, arguably the greatest opera composer ever, tried to recreate the totality of Greek drama in his huge *Ring* cycle, with results still resounding to this day.

In the 20th century Greek ideas also proved potently inspiring, in art, literature and philosophy. Martin Heidegger (1889–1976), among the century's most fundamental philosophers, grounded his radical thinking on Greek foundations, looking back partly to the Presocratics. Heidegger was the godfather of Existentialism, the century's most influential – or fashionable – philosophy. Ideas first aired by the Greeks seldom stay dead for long.

Below: In 1504 Michelangelo completed his heroic David, *the first truly gigantic nude statue since antiquity. It incarnates Hellenic ideals both of male beauty and democracy – that of the Florentine republic, which Michelangelo ardently supported.*

INDEX